D0239152

What's Age Got to Do with It?

Books by the same author:

Could it Be Dementia?: Losing Your Mind Doesn't Mean Losing Your Soul (Monarch Books, 2008)

Dementia: Frank and Linda's Story: New Understanding, New Approaches, New Hope (Monarch Books, 2010)

Worshipping with Dementia: Meditations, Scriptures and Prayers for Sufferers and Carers (Monarch Books, 2010)

Dementia: Pathways to Hope: Spiritual Insights and Practical Hope for Carers (Monarch Books, 2015)

WHAT'S
AGE
GOT TO DO
WITH IT?

*Living out God's purpose
at all ages*

Louise Morse

MONARCH
BOOKS

Published by Lion Books
an imprint of
Lion Hudson IP Ltd
Wilkinson House, Jordan Hill Road,
Oxford OX2 8DR, England
www.lionhudson.com/lion

ISBN 978 0 85721 748 6
e-ISBN 978 0 85721 749 3

First edition 2017

Acknowledgments
Every effort has been made to trace and contact copyright owners for material used in this book. We apologize for any inadvertent omissions or errors.
Extract from "Don't preach to us about ageism, change the law" by Terry Prone in *The Times* copyright © 2009, Terry Prone. Reprinted by permission of *The Times*.
Unless otherwise stated and where marked "NLT", Scripture quotations are taken from the Holy Bible, New Living Translation, copyright _ 1996, 2004. Used by permission of Tyndale House Publishers, Inc., Carol Stream, Illinois 60188. All rights reserved.
Scripture quotations marked "NASB" are taken from the New American Standard Bible Copyright © 1960, 1962, 1963, 1968, 1971, 1972, 1973, 1975, 1977, 1995 by The Lockman Foundation.
Scripture quotations marked "NKJV" are taken from the New King James Version®. Copyright © 1982 by Thomas Nelson, Inc. Used by permission. All rights reserved.
Scripture quotations marked "CJB" are taken from the Complete Jewish Bible, Copyright © 1998 by David H. Stern. All rights reserved.
Scripture quotations marked "ESV" are taken from The ESV® Bible (The Holy Bible, English Standard Version®), copyright © 2001 by Crossway, a publishing ministry of Good News Publishers. Used by permission. All rights reserved.
Scripture quotations marked "Amplified Bible" are taken from the Amplified® Bible (AMP), Copyright © 2015 by The Lockman Foundation. Used by permission. www. Lockman.org.
Scripture quotations marked "NIV" are taken from the Holy Bible, New International Version®, NIV® Copyright ©1973, 1978, 1984, 2011 by Biblica, Inc.® Used by permission. All rights reserved worldwide.
Scripture quotations marked "KJV" are taken from the Authorized (King James) Version: rights in the Authorized Version in the United Kingdom are vested in the Crown. Reproduced by permission of the Crown's patentee, Cambridge University Press.

A catalogue record for this book is available from the British Library

Printed and bound in the UK, October 2017, LH26

Contents

Acknowledgments

MY FIRST THANK YOU GOES to readers of my previous books, who have been so generous with their feedback and encouragement. Many have emailed or written, and many have gone out of their way to find me and chat at national Christian events. An example is the mother who whizzed by with her small daughter in a pushchair, saying as she went, "I can't stop – but wanted you to know that my mother read *Dementia: Frank and Linda's Story* and thought it was so good she bought 20 copies to give to people she thought it would help. The first copy went to our vicar."

"Why did she think that?" I asked.

Over a shoulder she said, "I'll come back and tell you later!" And she did. Then there was Allison, clutching a battered copy of *Worshipping with Dementia* with Post-it™ notes sticking out of the pages, asking, "When are you going to do another one? Because the residents in the care homes I go into love it." And the couple I met at a conference in North Wales (where the weather was so cold I kept imagining press stories headed, "Speaker Found Frozen to Death at Christian Conference"). The wife said she had cared for both her parents as they aged, and they had both developed dementia.

"It was reading your books that kept me going," she told me, "and when I knew this one was coming out I made my husband order it straight away."

"She stayed up half the night reading it," he added. It wasn't just the practical information, because that's available all over the place now; they said it was the scriptural, spiritual insight.

THANK YOU A MILLION TIMES to my colleagues at the Pilgrims' Friend Society (PFS). Thank you for sending me the information and the stories that you do; thank you for your comments on my pieces, and thank you for allowing me into your worlds. Thank you to Roger Hitchings, retired pastor, speaker and writer, and inspiration. And a very special THANK YOU for Janet Jacob, former psychogeriatric nurse and home manager, my friend and colleague who speaks with me at conference and is always calm and collected and – most of all – steadfast. Bless you, Janet! A huge THANK YOU, too, to my charity's chief executive, Stephen Hammersley. Sometimes it worries me that I find myself agreeing with everything Stephen suggests, because it hasn't always been that way with me and CEOs. But Stephen brings a huge array of God-given talents, especially the gift of enabling and encouraging.

Finally, authors' dedications probably don't usually mention the Holy Spirit, but I'd like to put on record my unending gratitude to Him who is still taking the "weak and foolish" (1 Corinthians 1:27) to reveal His wisdom to the world.

Preface

Grow old along with me!
The best is yet to be,
The last of life, for which the first was made:
Our times are in His Hand
Who saith "A whole I planned,
Youth shows but half; trust God: see all, nor be afraid!"
(From *Rabbi Ben Ezra*, by Robert Browning)

There is a story of a man who nearly drowned in a sinking ship because his cabin door was locked. After frantically pushing and rattling the door handle, he suddenly realized that it wasn't locked at all, and he managed to escape. He had simply been pushing the door away from him instead of pulling it towards him. Is this what we've been doing when it comes to unlocking the vision of all that God intends for us in our latter years? Have we been so panicked by thoughts of ageing that we have been pushing away from us the "the best for which the first was made"?

When He created the universe, God set in motion times and seasons and the ageing process. Old age was part of His plan from the beginning – that people should ripen to maturity, developing wisdom through a lifetime of experience and relationship with Him, eventually taking their place as elders in society. Robert Browning saw it, and so do others, including many world-leading experts on old age. Dr William H. Thomas, a gerontologist and professor at the University of Maryland, wrote an award-winning book that has been hailed as "a seminal work and a call to arms".[1] It's called *What Are Old People For? How Elders Will Save the World*. He believes that now is the time to restore "elderhood".

An even more authoritative book, the Bible, describes God's plan for older people with crystal clarity. A ripe old age is regarded in the Bible as one of the greatest blessings to be bestowed upon mankind, not just for the individual but for the whole of society. "They are the glue that holds society together," said a survey published by the RVS (formerly the WRVS) that detailed the economic and human contribution of older people.

Most people reading this book will be Bible readers, and many will actively study it. So how is it that we haven't seen the richness of God's plan for us in old age? William Thomas says that it is because we have been blinded by a "malign adulation of adulthood" and the belief that it is the peak of human development. It was a mindset generated by the Baby Boomers, the largest generation in history, which, because of its sheer weight of numbers, became a crucible for change. As a result, we have unconsciously absorbed a "declinist" view of old age that not only fails to see its purpose but has taken against it, tarnishing it with soul-destroying ageism. Ageism has so permeated our thinking and decimated our expectations that, instead of making the most of old age and the elderhood God designed for us, we lock ourselves into a notion of perpetual adulthood. The anti-ageing industry is raking in billions. Looking on the "outward appearance" (1 Samuel 16:7), we fail to see the inner qualities of older people, those who have been "ripened" and refined, as God intended.

But the tide is turning. Among the ripples are warnings from business gurus that employers need to drop ageist attitudes and recognize the value of their older employees, changing their practices in order to retain them. And like a rustling in the treetops (2 Samuel 5:24) are the stories of how many older people are living out God's purposes in old age, sometimes quite magnificently. The stories in the following pages will show how, even in their 100s, they are following God's plan, blessing and encouraging others as well as themselves.

There are treasures waiting for us in old age. Yes, there can be physical frailty, but the real person, the "inner man" that is destined for eternal life, is being strengthened and transformed. Psychologist James Hillman wrote:

> "... let us entertain the idea that character requires the additional years and that the long last of life is forced upon us neither by genes nor by conservational medicine nor by societal collusion. The last years conform and fulfil character."[2]

Make no mistake: God designed old age deliberately. Each older person is here for a purpose, for those "good works" that God has equipped him or her to do (Ephesians 2:10). Among those who are just getting on with it is Douglas Higgins, an evangelical Christian who wrote a book at the age of 100 as a testimony to win others to Christ, because he says he is too weak to stand and give talks any more.[3]

Psalm 92: 12–15 (NLT) says:

> But the godly will flourish like palm trees
> and grow strong like the cedars of Lebanon.

For they are transplanted to the Lord's own house.
They flourish in the courts of our God.
Even in old age they will still produce fruit;
they will remain vital and green.
They will declare, "The Lord is just!
He is my rock!
There is no evil in Him!"

We need to up our expectations of old age, both for ourselves and for others, for, as far as God's plan is concerned, age has everything to do with it.

Chapter 1

Steady the Seniors – Our Day is Coming!

Leaving the gym this morning, I saw that the manager's door was open and popped my head around to ask if he'd take part in my survey.

"Sure, come in," he answered; "are you going to use shorthand again?" This tells you that he's intrigued by shorthand and that I've surveyed him before. His observations are valuable because he sees quite a few hundred people over time, observing their progress and enthusiasm and, from the records, knows how old they are.

My question was simple. "I'm writing a book about people and old age, and want to ask – when do you think old age begins?"

He thought a bit. "That's a hard one to answer," he said. "We have people here from 17 upwards. Sometimes people in their 40s and 50s can seem older than others in their 80s. They have a kind of tired air about them. I think everything depends on a person's attitude – their motivation, everything."

Our view of when we become old is changing. When asked, people usually say ten years ahead of their own age. It may sound trite, but it is true that we are as old as we feel. "Why old age starts at 85" was the title of a newspaper article in March 2016. British pensioners are pushing back the age barrier, it said, with many not considering themselves elderly until they reach the age of 85. And one in ten surveyed said that old age started at the age of 90. Unlike previous generations, those between 60 and 69 did not see themselves as old at all, and two-thirds of them were planning to do something they had never done before.

One of my favourite newspaper clippings is the story of 105-year-old Sheila Thompson, pictured at the wheel of her car.[4] The story begins, "When Sheila Thompson was born in 1902 few believed these new-fangled motor cars would ever be a serious alternative to the horse-drawn carriage." It goes on to say she is hoping she won't lose her driving licence after a slight prang with another car. She said, "I had been at church and the street is very narrow there. A man was loading things into his car but was doing it with the door open on the road side and I came along and hit it." In another newspaper she's reported as saying that if she lost her licence she wouldn't be able to take the "old folk" to church. Mrs Thompson had great motivation!

To a large extent, motivation depends on our expectations. We expect that things will turn out well, or that we'll achieve our goals. If we don't we're unlikely to move towards them. And our expectations spring largely from our life experience, which, in turn, shapes our view of ourselves. Children who are raised by parents who tell them they are valued and have the potential to achieve much will become adults who believe in themselves and their abilities. They see possibilities in life. An example is Michael "Eddie" Edwards, who believed he could be a British Olympic skiing champion. His mother believed in him, too, and at one point sacrificed the family car and savings to help him. Michael didn't fit the standard skiing champion pattern at all. He came from an inner-city, working-class family, with no experience of or even holidays in the Alps. But against all the odds – coming from the wrong side of the tracks with no contacts, no money, and no coach – he did it. He became the British ski jumping champion. His Wikipedia entry says:

Eddie "The Eagle" Edwards is a British skier and ski jumper who in 1988 became the first competitor to represent Great Britain in Olympic ski jumping. At the time, he was the British ski jumping record holder, the world number nine in amateur speed skiing, (106.8 mph (171.9 km/h) and the stunt jumping world record holder. Finishing last in the 70m and 90m events, he became famous as an example of an underdog or "heroic failure", and of perseverance and achievement without funding. In 2016, he was portrayed by Taron Egerton in the biographical film *Eddie the Eagle*, co-starring Hugh Jackman as fictional coach Bronson Peary.

Another story of motivation spurred by burning belief is that of Stuart Wilson, an archaeology graduate living in Monmouth, South Wales. He was convinced that a field in nearby Trellech covered the remains of a medieval town. He'd noticed that as moles burrowed beneath the farmer's field they threw up fragments of what appeared to be medieval pottery. He also suspected, from the field layout, that it had been overlaid onto an existing pattern. He was so convinced of the hidden archaeological treasure in the field that, in shades of Matthew 13:44, he spent £32,000 on buying the field instead of putting a deposit on his own house. For 15 years, he and a hardy band of volunteers worked painstakingly in the field until they finally unearthed what they believe are the remains of a sprawling medieval city.

After years of scepticism from the archaeological community, Stuart Wilson is now being taken seriously. He has even been invited by the Cardiff Archaeological Society to speak at Cardiff University. He says, "People thought I was mad and really I should have bought a house rather than a field. But it turned out to be the best decision of my life. I don't regret it at all."[5]

If we were all living the way that God intended, we would be encouraging one another and building one another up (1 Thessalonians 5:11). We would be devoted to one another, even preferring others over ourselves (Romans 12:5–10). If we're honest, we would say that as Christians we get near this ideal only a fraction of the time. And in life in general – in business, in shopping, competing for a parking space, and all those things that make up daily living, we see very little of it. But because God planned life so that we would develop in relationship with others in a reciprocal way, we form our core beliefs about ourselves and our abilities in response to the way others treat us.

It's why we are told to guard our heart, "for it is the source of life's consequences". Proverbs 4:23 is expressed well in the Complete Jewish Bible. What we believe in our hearts directs our thinking, our attitude, our expectations, and our behaviour.

So what's age got to do with it?

Our core beliefs are even more important as we get older – especially *now*. Because we are tipping over the cusp of one of the most fundamental changes in society, one that will elevate the status of older people and release their potential to the benefit of *all* – if we get it right. It's not a time for saying, "Older people rule, yay!" but for holding steady to our beliefs and having our hearts grounded in Christ. It's also time to clear away ageism and age discrimination, which is like pollution, lurking unseen, everywhere. A small example is when it comes to looking for a job. Although it is illegal for employers to discriminate on the basis of age, psychologists from the University of Kent found recently that they are more likely to select candidates who describe themselves with characteristics typical of younger people. Older vocabulary includes "careful" and "considerate" and "understanding others' views and settling arguments", whereas that of younger ones included "creative" and "IT-literate".

It's wrong, it has to change, and it is going to change, according to Dr William H. Thomas, a graduate of Harvard Medical School. Dr Thomas is an international authority on geriatric medicine and eldercare. In a riveting TED Talk he said, "I actually accept ageing. I endorse ageing – because it is ageing that is going to save us." (Google William H. Thomas, YouTube.)

For the first time in history, we can expect to live to our 80s, 90s, or 100s, or even more. If current clinical trials of the repurposing for older people of an old drug that has improved the health of people with diabetes are successful, we could live to be 120. If that should happen, it's not unreasonable to suppose that we would expect to go on working until we were 100: we are already seeing the age that state pensions are paid being pushed back in the UK.

It's an extraordinary development. "More years were added to life expectancy in the 20th century than all years added across all prior millennia of human evolution combined," says Laura Carstensen, Professor of Psychology and Professor in Public

Policy at Stanford University. (Google her name to hear her talk on YouTube.)

She also believes that older people have qualities that are an immense benefit to all ages. "Older people are more positive in their outlook and less inclined to negativity, have increased knowledge and expertise, are more given to reconciliation than confrontation, and have better-balanced emotional lives," she says. Criminality decreases with age, as do stress, worry, and anger. Study after study shows that older people are happier than middle-aged or younger people. Older people do not take unnecessary risks. "You don't go on blind dates after the age of 50," she says with a smile. Trading-floor dealer Nick Leeson was only 26 when he caused the collapse of the 223-year-old Barings Bank, and many financial experts believe that if there had been more mature investment bankers in the lead-up to the financial crash of 2008, it wouldn't have happened.

In America, the word "seniors" is often used for older people. An English colleague says it isn't the right word to use, because it implies that older people have seniority, a status accorded to higher rank, or longer service or employment. But that's what Dr Carstensen seems to be implying, and it is also what the Bible says. When Paul wrote to Titus (Titus 2) about teaching sound doctrine, he also showed how it should be done: "Teach the older men to exercise self-control, to be worthy of respect, and to live wisely. They must have sound faith...," he said, and, "These older women must train the younger women," outlining a cascading programme for the fellowship, which started from a senior position. I like the word "senior" and would like to see it used more often.

Dr William Thomas also sees older people as seniors but has another name for it – elderhood. "Elderhood is real," he insists. "It's rich and deep and meaningful and it can be yours." But to obtain it you have to be willing to outgrow adulthood. It sounds odd, put that way, but he means that you have to eschew all the anti-ageing products and gizmos and admit that your body is growing old.

Here he reveals one of the modern drivers of ageism, which he roundly denounces. The reason that it exists at all is a "design fault", he believes. Not in creation, but in the way we have designed our concept of the progression of life. We are compelled to accept that life has three stages – we are children, or adolescents, or adults. That's it – no old age.

Since the last world war the life cycle itself has been changing. About 60 years ago we saw the emergence of an "enormous" generation, one with more people than any generation in history. The people born just after the war became known as the Baby Boomer generation. As they grew older, because of their immense numbers, they had the power to bend our culture, and not only bend the culture but magnify the stage of life that they, the Boomers, occupied. For example, "in the 1950s adolescence was seen as a quirky period where everyone had teenage problems before they grew up. Fifteen years later that massive generation slammed into adolescence. They created their first generational crucible.

"Then they moved out of adolescence and discovered adulthood and all of a sudden youthful rebellion didn't look quite so nice. Playtime was over... the humdrum qualities of predictability and reliability and performance were magnified and became cardinal virtues."

When Boomers began inhabiting the centre stage of adulthood, they became massive consumers of business efficiency books and manuals.

Dr Thomas said, "We magnified adulthood so real adults take pride in how busy they are. We love the smell of electrons in the morning because they smell like victory. We've got hyper-active, hyper-kinetic adulthood.

"We've been told that the problem is ageing. But that's wrong. Ageing is not the problem. It's our obsession with youth. Our excessive devotion to the virtues of youthful adulthood. It is youth that is throwing our lives out of balance. We are living in a society afflicted by a malignant enlargement of adulthood."

Just as the Boomer generation dropped the values of adolescence for those of adulthood, now they are growing closer each day to the next stage of the life cycle. Dr Thomas finds the prospect exciting, even though it means that millions of them are denying the reality of their own ageing. Sales of anti-ageing products show a burning desire to avoid life's next developmental challenge. But still it will come, and he is glad. Because as this huge, influential post-war generation leave adulthood, they're going to begin finding out that there's life "out there", and it's not as they know it!

So, just as the Baby Boomers created a generational "crucible" when they were younger, Dr Thomas sees this happening again as they leave adulthood and become "elders". The inference is that as the "malignant enlargement of adulthood" deflates, there will be an enlargement of "elderhood", which might cause us to reshape the concept of the human life cycle and, in the process, eliminate ageism. Quite simply, these Baby Boomers, powerful because of their numbers and their non-conformist attitude, will reinvent the concept of old age. Dr Thomas concludes, "Our society needs elders. We inhabit a society that is run by adults. Without elder supervision. Now is the time for us to begin rebuilding our life cycle."

It's an exciting prospect, not just because it will acknowledge the special qualities of seniors but because it moves the pattern of life back to the way God designed it to be. It's always interesting when secular knowledge catches up with biblical wisdom. Ageing is part of our humanity and God intended, from the beginning, that the qualities of older people would make life better for *all*.

When older people were valued it happened naturally, because they were listened to with respect. Stories illustrating this are found all through the Bible, from the beginning to the end. An example is in the letter written by the apostle Paul from prison to his friend Philemon. Philemon lived in Colossae and was a member of the Colossian church, having been led to faith by Paul. Now Paul is persuading Philemon to take back his runaway slave, Onesimus, whom Paul had met and brought to Christ while in prison. Paul knew full well that in the culture of the day Philemon had the right to have Onesimus executed, but Paul appeals to him as a brother in Christ and a partner in the gospel, and for "love's sake" (Philemon 9). He also appeals as "Paul, the *aged*, and now also a prisoner of Jesus Christ" (my italics). He is not presenting himself as an old man looking for sympathy, but a *senior*, to whom deference is due.

Looking back on his days of eminence as a civic leader, Job recalled, "The young stepped aside when they saw me, and even the aged rose in respect at my coming" (Job 29:8, NLT). *Even the aged rose* when Job entered the room! It tells us how highly elderhood was respected in Old Testament times.

I've been trying to picture what a society like this would look like. One where seniors are empowered and engaged, where they live to their full potential. Where they are asked to give their testimonies in church on a Sunday morning as part of the worship service, and are a normal part of all decision making, including the balance of the worship music. Where they are valued as highly as God values them: *where age has everything to do with it*. I had a glimpse of it in a conversation a few weeks ago with a couple in their early sixties, from Uganda.

We were sitting over breakfast at a Christian conference, and began to talk about the church in Uganda and the church here in the UK, where they've lived for over 20 years. We also talked about how they met. They'd had a fairly long friendship before their relationship began to deepen. They told me how the older men in their church in Uganda were mentors for the younger and how, before proposing marriage, William had had several conversations with his mentor. Then the mentor approached Judith, and told her that William was thinking of asking her to marry him. I thought how kind that was, and how much pressure it took off the suitor and how much he had been helped by the experience and the listening ear of the older man.

In the chapters to come, we'll be looking at this new age of "elderhood" and how we can reshape the concept of the life cycle by applying the Designer's original template. We'll also look at ways of preparing for it. As Christians, we mustn't be passive and let elderhood slip away from us. Our world is changing, and we want to affect some of those changes. It's as the cabin crew say as the plane is about to roll down the runway: "Fasten your seat belts and prepare for take-off." We need to be fastened to the Scriptures, not just because we are going to new heights but because we can be the pacesetters.

Chapter 2
The Real Life Design

Some time ago I bought a new kind of can opener for an elderly relative who was having difficulty using the old butterfly type that she'd had for years. The new one was designed to suspend the can and remove the cap, hands-free, at the press of a button. I took it out of the box and stood it on the kitchen table, intending to try it out, but for the life of me couldn't see how it worked. I held it upside down and turned it round and round, but all I saw was a small shape dangling from a solid black object that reminded me of the enigmatic "Thing" that communicated to spacecraft in Terry Pratchett's series "The Nome Trilogy". I was fishing inside the box for the leaflet, muttering about having to have instructions for a can opener these days, for goodness' sake, when in from school came my 13-year-old grandson.

"Wossup?" he asked.

"It's this thing," I answered. "I can't see how it works so I'm looking for the instruction leaflet."

"You don't need that," he said, picking it up and turning the top around. "Look, this bit slots in there and the can goes in there and you turn this here." He's now 17 and planning to be an engineer, and if he's anything like his grandfathers, who were both engineers in different fields, he will be designing things that fit together, and probably writing instructions for their use and maintenance.

People seem to fall into two different camps when it comes to equipment and instructions. There are those who read the instructions first, and those who read the instructions as they put it together. There's also a third group, of people like me, who read the instructions first and also as they go along, and still have to refer to them again from time to time. It doesn't help when the item has been produced in China or Japan and the manual has been translated into English by a native speaker.

But, when it comes to understanding God's design for our lives, we simply have to read the Designer's manual, the Bible. It shows us how to put our lives together and how to help others do the same, daily maintenance and repairs, and how to put them back together again when they fall apart. It was inspired by the Holy Spirit (2 Timothy 3:16), and has been translated into nearly every language so that everyone can read it. It lays out the real life plan, the one designed by the Creator Himself. The why, the how, the reason for our being, and the progression of life from birth to old age are all there; guidance and precise direction, just for the reading.

It describes different stages of life and gives directions for each one. We're told how to bring up children, how to live as we're growing up, how to live as adults and when we are old, and even how to die. There's no sense that adulthood is the peak of the design and that we should hurry into it and stay there as long as possible. It's sad that children are being encouraged to be adults instead of enjoying their childhood. It makes me cringe to see children of less than 12 years of age singing adult songs about emotions they can't possibly understand, or taking part in beauty competitions complete with heels and make-up.

In schools, children are now being taught about "gender issues" when they shouldn't really be thinking about gender but about climbing trees and scrumping apples and collecting tadpoles.

Old age, a blessing from God

The Bible has a good deal to say about old age. God's life design does not throw in old age as a sorry tail end that has to be endured through decline and senility: on the contrary, it could be argued that, psychologically and spiritually, older people represent the pinnacle of the life cycle – a time of completion, of fruition, of learning, and of knowing God. There can be physical weaknesses in an ageing body, but the "inner man", the essence of the person that will live for ever, is growing and developing. The Jewish Torah describes Abraham as one who "grew old and came along in days" (Genesis 24:1), and these accumulated days, each replete with learning and achievement, meant that with the passing of each one his worth increased. Thus, a ripe old age is regarded as one of the greatest blessings to be bestowed upon mankind. It was seen as a blessing from God. "I will reward them with a long life and give them my salvation" is the promise in Psalm 91:16 (NLT).

The life design applies whether we are Christian believers or not. We can't opt out by saying "I don't believe that; therefore it doesn't apply to me", because the evidence shows that it does. Jesus didn't come to impose a moral code on humanity, which we were not made for, observed preacher and writer Selwyn Hughes. No: Jesus came to reveal the nature of Reality itself. "He lifted up the laws of effective living which are written into the universe and into every nerve and tissue of our being, and showed us that there is just no other way to live."[6]

It's intriguing to think that at the heart of our economy is a simple precept of divine design – that we make a living by serving one another. Whether it's in retail, business to business, research, or teaching, the principle is the same. And the more we serve, the more engaged with life we become and the more satisfaction we obtain. Bill and Melinda Gates are among the richest people in the world, yet they work actively to make life better for people in poor countries – and it's not something they do just from the comfort of an air-conditioned office. They take themselves into quite primitive situations at times to speak to people there, gauge local needs, and see how their solutions are working. Instead of just giving and standing back, they make sure that their projects produce results and their talents and experience in analysis and systems must be of huge value.

No one can hold back the physical ageing process, although there are serious attempts that can cost huge amounts of money. When and how we age is written into our very being, in our genetic inheritance, in our DNA. We see that Jesus experienced ageing, and "increased in wisdom and in stature and in favour with God and man" (Luke 2:52, KJV). And no one can deny that we accumulate learning and experience day by day.

Jewish tradition agrees roughly with our current view of the stages of old age, namely that there is "young old", which includes people newly retired, say between 65 and 80, "middle-stage old", between 80 and 90, and after that, "old old", going up to 100 and more. It's a gracious design that allows a gradual acceptance of the shift from "doing" to "being", as physical energies decline and we move from an external landscape to one that is internal. It's a time of reflecting, of leaning into Jesus.

Learning to "be" rather than "do" can be very difficult for people who have lived very active lives, especially those who've contributed much. Evangelists Billy Graham and John Stott both said that they had been taught about death but not about how to be old. When he moved into one of our sheltered housing apartments, retired pastor and author Clifford Pond found the transition difficult to make, and wrote an article for our magazine about dealing with loneliness and drawing ever closer to God. Perhaps reflecting actress Bette Davis's sentiment that "old age ain't no place for sissies", Jeff Lucas, author and teaching pastor of the large Timberline Church in Colorado, commented, "Nobody told me anything about the one thing you never believe will happen when you're young but happens to every human on the planet. And that is that we will all grow old."

The Fall means we're down, but not out

After the Fall, death came into the lives of men and women and their relationship with God changed. The coming of death introduced the process of decay that we define today as ageing. But, although it was a judgment from God, in His kindness He allowed life to continue to be a process of development and maturing. It's as the apostle Paul says: "The outer man is decaying but the inner is being changed from one degree of glory to another" (2 Corinthians 4:16).

We are not going to see any signs of physical decay in heaven. I think there is a time in young adulthood when human beings are at their most beautiful. Perhaps we will be at the peak of our beauty and at the same time spiritually mature in heaven. We will all be perfect, though, because the Bible tells us we will be like Him (1 John 3:2). We will have been changed to our fullest "degree of glory".

One effect of ageism is that we can fail to see this "inner being" in God's older saints. We tend to look easily at the external, missing the real person inside. A senior nurse in one of our homes once said to me, "It makes me cross when someone sees Winifred tottering along the corridor with her walking frame and says, 'Poor old thing'. I want to say, 'No!' This is Winifred who helped deliver hundreds of babies in the Congo." In contrast was an email from one of our trustees who had attended the funeral of someone he knew I was particularly fond of. He wrote about its being a glorious funeral, a time of rejoicing because everyone knew she had said, quite vigorously, how much she longed to be Home.

We will not be perfected this side of heaven, yet there are biblical descriptions that paint a picture: "They still bear fruit in old age; they are ever full of sap and green" (Psalm 92:14, ESV). Galatians (5:22–23) describes the fruit of the Spirit as love, joy, peace, patience, kindness, goodness, faithfulness, gentleness, and self-control. I'm writing in a Christian context and am aware that this is God's ideal, and that the goals that the Bible sets out are not completely attainable while we are living on earth but are there to draw us onwards and upwards. At every stage of our life we have a choice to make, whether to do it God's way or not. We can progress to "proven character" (Romans 5:4), or remain less than God intends for us. The fruit of the Spirit in an older person is an absolute delight.

An example is Constance, who was 81 when I met her in one of our care homes. She'd been born to missionaries in Java (then the Dutch East Indies), and qualified as a pharmacist in England. Working in the north, she met a Czech evangelist who had escaped from Dachau and had been one of the preachers in the famous "Isles and Scottish" revival. After his death she became a hospital chaplain and used to take services at the care home, before ill health meant she herself needed residential care. When we met she was radiating "the fragrance of Christ", and organizing a regular weekly Bible study. A carer at the home told me how he'd given his life to the Lord through her teaching. Constance was an unusually beautiful lady, and I often thought how her gentle spirit had shaped her face through her life.

People who work with elderly Christians will tell you that even when they are very frail and weak, they are *fruitful*. Catriona, a pastor for the elderly in a large church in Birmingham, said that sometimes one will say to her, "Oh, I'm no use now. I'm hopeless at praying", and Catriona will say, "No, you are not. Your thoughts, your sighs are your prayers. When you think of someone, lift that person to God in your mind." Roger Hitchings, a retired pastor who has worked with older people for years in different capacities, remembers being taken by his mother to visit an old man who couldn't afford to heat his whole house, so lived in just one room. Although he had so little, however, he had learned to lean more and more on Jesus, and Roger remembers how he radiated contentment.

"More" is a good adverb for older people. In Cambridge, England, people ride bikes or catch buses to work rather than drive cars because the ancient town is small and impassable and the car parks outrageously expensive. I caught buses more in Cambridge than at any other time in my life, and found myself one day sitting alongside an older lady, probably in her 80s, who was going back to the same village. She'd just attended a conference on growing old. This was years before thoughts of old age had even entered my mind, but I've always remembered one thing she said, the thing she'd learned that had impressed her most of all. She'd been told, she said, that when you're older you're the same as you've always been, only more so. Including, I ventured, more interesting?

"It depends," she replied; "if you're a self-centred boring young person you'll become a self-centred boring old person."

One of the things Christians can be grateful for is that God intends to change us, to make us more like Jesus. In addition, thank God, He doesn't leave it to us, or we'd never get there. He empowers us: "For God is working in you, giving you the desire and the power to do what pleases Him" (Philippians 2:13). Being a Christian doesn't mean conforming to an outward form of beliefs and behaviour; it means being transformed inwardly. It was a blessing to listen to a successful property developer, who was planning a retirement village in a lovely part of the country, saying with a passion that his main aim in life was to press on to become like Jesus (Romans 8:29).

God's design creates growth

Experience can't be bottled, or taught – it has to be lived. You don't know as much at 40 as you do at 80 and, contrary to the ageist view, studies show that our crystalline intelligence, that is the ability to use learned knowledge and experience, gets better as we age. You may get wrinkly on the outside, but you're getting stronger and wiser in the *real* you – the you that will live for ever. If there are mirrors in heaven, we will be amazed at ourselves. Or perhaps we will look and think, "That's how I was always meant to be!"

"While youth is beautiful – wondrously beautiful – age has a beauty and a majesty all its own; and that, although those who are at the beginning of life may acquire much knowledge, those who are nearing its close may possess that wisdom which is knowledge applied," wrote Henry Durbanville in a precious little booklet, *The Best is Yet To Be*, first published in 1950.[7]

God has so designed the life cycle that the longer people live, the more they learn through experience and the more wisdom they accumulate. Living to old age creates the qualities that God intended to benefit the rest of society: those that psychologist Laura Carstensen and Dr William Thomas (and others) say must be recognized and "released" for the benefit of us all. Psychologist James Hillman wrote:

> ... let us entertain the idea that character requires the additional years and that the long last of life is forced upon us neither by genes nor by conservational medicine nor by societal collusion. The last years conform and fulfil character.[8]

But this fulfilled character is not acknowledged because scientific theories about ageing all accept, without question, the doctrine of the perfection of youth. Yet, as Thomas observes, "We possess culture because our ancestors had the wisdom to distinguish vigour from value. They saw, as we so often do not, beyond mere physical strength and grasped the virtues hidden within the necessity of growing old."[9]

When it comes to older people, the focus is on decline and little heed, if any, is given to the steady emergence of new gifts and capacities. Sadly, this thinking has permeated even people who do know the Father's life design, those of us who love the Bible. We are like potatoes, dug into secular soil and unconsciously taking in its values by osmosis. The media showers us with ageist messages day after day, and we have absorbed them to the point that they have become part of our core beliefs. As a result, the view we have built of old age is often grey and gloomy and it colours our expectations for ourselves and for others.

When I or one of my colleagues take a seminar on using God-given talents in old age, people in the audience often reflect them back to us in dozens of little ways. At the beginning of our talks they're usually negative. "I don't want to be a burden…" is the most common refrain. A 50-year-old was describing his church's evangelistic work and I asked how they reached older people.

"Why would we do that – what would they bring?" he replied. He was an intelligent, middle-aged man I knew in a professional context. I was so stumped by his reply I was almost lost for words.

I ventured, "Wisdom, availability, willingness, a listening ear, ideas, collaboration?" He simply couldn't see it. This good-natured, pleasant man couldn't see it.

"I thought my useful days were finished," said a lively 70-year-old retired teacher. And when someone suspects they might be developing an illness or disability they will say, "But what can I expect at my age?"

Yet experts say that healthspan is increasing along with lifespan, so we now have the largest, healthiest older generation in history. And it's one that's growing all the time. We have more of the qualities of elderhood around us than ever before. "The situation is not unlike that of a host who lays out a feast for the guests and then insists that the food is spoilt and the wine gone rancid," writes William Thomas.[10] "It is like adults sitting before a banquet, not daring to eat or drink."

If you've read C. S. Lewis's *The Last Battle* you'll remember the part where Aslan tries to persuade the dwarfs hiding in the darkness of the barn that there is sunshine and life all around them. He shakes his mane, and "instantly a glorious feast appeared on the dwarfs' knees; pies and tongues and pigeons and trifles and ices, and each dwarf had a goblet of good wine in his hand". But the dwarfs couldn't see them or taste them. One thought he was eating hay and another an old turnip, and the rich, red wine in the goblets tasted to them like dirty water out of a donkey's drinking trough.

The doctrine of ageing

Is there a biblical doctrine on ageing? Doctrine is important, because it is a statement of beliefs that are taught and accepted by the church. We're familiar with the doctrine of salvation, justification by faith alone, the basics of Scripture, honouring one's parents, and the call to live a holy life. But it's been put to me that there is no doctrine on ageing. So I asked Roger Hitchings, who has far greater theological knowledge than I have, and he said that isn't the case: there is a clear set of teachings running through the Bible that can be set out accurately as a theology of old age. That no one has brought all this teaching together in a structured way is a huge gap in the whole area of pastoral theology that needs to be filled, and I understand that it's something Roger is currently working on.

Roger explains, "The biblical doctrine of ageing begins in Genesis with statements about the length of individuals' lives, showing that how long we live is significant and how we are to use those days. It is developed through passages like Leviticus 18 and Exodus 20. The concept of honouring parents is refined to older people and widows in particular, see for instance Proverbs 1 – 7 where an old man puts together advice for his son. The examples and practices of old men like Abraham, Jacob, and Moses, to name just a few, all set out a doctrinal framework for understanding how we are to approach ageing. Further definition is given in Psalms 71 and 92, Isaiah 46, and Isaiah 41:4, and many other passages in Scripture, and the emphasis on generations is all part of the theology of ageing."

Time to enjoy God

Several studies find that seniors are happier than younger people, and experience joy in their lives, a point made by Laura Carstensen in her TED Talk.[11] It was interesting to read comments on the YouTube page posted by younger people who simply could not believe that older people can be happy and have joy. It simply doesn't fit their "miserable" concept of old age.

One of the pleasures that God has kept for seniors is the time to sit, to be, and to count your blessings in ways you haven't had time for before. There's a worship song called "To Be in Your Presence" (Noel Richards, 1993), extolling the blessing of just resting in the presence of the Lord, cherishing each moment and not rushing away, rather like the young Joshua, who used to linger in God's presence after Moses left the Tent of Meeting. In the move from doing to being, seniors can delight in spending time with Him, focusing on Him, and enjoying Him. As adults there's so much pressure to do this and do that and accomplish a heap of good things, and it can make us feel that we have no time, even if we have. Older people have the gift of time.

Spending time with God was at the front of Reb Tevye's mind in *Fiddler on the Roof*, when he suggested that He might consider making him a rich man. He said he would enjoy seeing his wife, Golde, looking like a rich man's wife "with a proper double chin", and he'd build a big house with a staircase going up and one going down and one going nowhere, just for show. But most of all, if he were a rich man, Tevye would have time to sit in the synagogue and pray, and "maybe have a seat by the Eastern wall," and to "discuss the holy books with the learned men, several hours every day. That would be the sweetest thing of all".

In God's plan, age has everything to do with it

To sum up briefly, God built ageing into the universe. Old age, and older people, are here on purpose. God designed older people so that, at the end of a long life, they would radiate His faithfulness and His power to mould and change, and keep safe. They are like the Sherpas in the Himalayas, people who've climbed the mountain and are the best guides. Thomas Scharf, Professor of Social Gerontology at Newcastle University, says that evidence shows that civic life is sustained by engaged, much older people. "Without them, the rest of us would be even more atomised and work would dominate life even more strongly than it does," he adds. Best of all, God planned this time of life so seniors would have the time to grow closer to Him, and, as the Westminster Catechism puts it, "Enjoy him forever".

Robert Browning reflects the completeness of old age in his poem *Rabbi Ben Ezra*:

> *Grow old along with me!*
> *The best is yet to be,*
> *The last of life, for which the first was made;*
> *Our times are in His Hand*
> *Who saith, "A whole I planned,*
> *Youth shows but half; trust God: see all, nor be afraid!"*

Chapter 3
Clearing the Runway

Knowing God's purpose for your life is a great incentive for going forward. But before we can take off and fly, the runway has to be cleared of obstructions.

One of the fastest and most beautiful planes ever to fly was Concorde. It could fly at twice the speed of sound and would get from London to New York in three and a half hours. People used to say that you could fly to the States in the morning, do a day's business, and fly back before the pubs closed. Concorde would take off and land literally like a bird, with its long, graceful nose high, wings swept back like a swan's and at an angle that made the wheels seem slightly forward.

"You would always stop what you were doing," said Brian Lovegrove, a former British Airways employee, of Concorde take-offs and landings. "You could never have enough of seeing it. It was a delight to watch and hear."[12] It was the sleekest, most technologically advanced plane on earth, and it graced the skies for 27 years. Then, in January 2002, during take-off from Charles de Gaulle Airport, the front right tyre of the left landing gear ran over a strip of metal that had fallen from another aircraft. The debris was thrown against the wing structure, rupturing a fuel tank and causing a major fire under the left wing. The crew wrestled the crippled jet into the air, but lost control moments later and crashed into a hotel. All 109 passengers and crew were killed, together with four people on the ground. Normal protocol for a Concorde flight included a full runway inspection before take-off; this was not completed (perhaps because the flight was already delayed by an hour). In the coming months and years there were reports about compounding factors, but, without any doubt, the debris on the runway was the primary cause.

And who could ever forget the day in January 2009 when a flock of birds were sucked into the engines of US Flight 1549 three minutes after take-off from LaGuardia Airport? Pilots Captain Chesley "Sully" Sullenberger and First Officer Jeffrey Skiles glided the plane to a safe landing in the Hudson River, and all 155 people on board survived. It's been called the Miracle on the Hudson.

A relatively small strip of debris on the runway stopped Concorde taking flight; birds being sucked into the engines brought down the US Airways Airbus A320: their power and purpose impeded by seemingly small things – which is exactly how ageism affects older people.

Before I began researching for this book, I thought that ageism was simply a sort of offhand humour that wasn't kind but did little harm. The longer and the more deeply I looked, the more I realized how invidious and pervasive it is – and how we are all affected by it to some degree. It comes in the form of obstacles that are (often unthinkingly) put in our way by others, or, like the birds in the engine, negative thoughts that fly into our minds and disempower us.

So what exactly is ageism?

The term was coined in 1968 by Dr Robert Butler, a psychiatrist and social activist. He said that just as racism and sexism are based on ethnicity and gender, ageism is a stereotyping of – and discrimination against – people simply because they are old. It is a social evil that should be outlawed, he averred. "Ageism: Another form of bigotry" is the title of a chapter in his book *The Longevity Revolution*, published in 2008.[13] It is still the most socially condoned form of prejudice in the world and remains one of the most institutionalized forms of prejudice today. "An ageist younger generation sees older people as different from itself; it subtly ceases to identify with its elders as human beings," noted Dr Butler.[14]

William Thomas attributes ageism to the "malign enlargement of adulthood"; the constant adulation of simply being an adult, producing and consuming and being a master of the universe, to the exclusion of others who don't belong. But there are deeper reasons, say an international group of professors who study it in detail. They are part of an organization called No to Ageism. They continually examine its history and causes, assess the consequences, and plan effective interventions to target it. (Their website, http://notoageism.com, is well worth a visit.)

Underlying ageism, say the professors, is a basic human desire to distance ourselves from any reminder of our inevitable death. In our society, people tend to associate old age with death and, therefore, being physically close to older people or even thinking about them tends to evoke "death anxiety". Their view chimes with that of Butler, who wrote, "People are afraid, and that leads to profound ambivalence." But he also added that "behind ageism is corrosive narcissism, the inability to accept our fate".

Political journalist Rachel Sylvester, writing in *The Times*, said that we want to imagine ourselves forever young, rather than admitting that one day we could become frail and fragile: "Old age is too close to death, the last taboo." So politicians make a platform of promising to save the National Health Service, which is about maintaining health, rather than pledging to salvage social care, which is about managing its decline.[15]

The "push away" factor was confirmed by a Princeton University study, which found that younger adults disliked older people attempting to look and behave younger than their years – in other words, they should keep their distance![16] They should not try to identify with us!

Daniel Read, Professor of Behavioural Science at Warwick Business School, says that people are unable to envisage an older "them" as they look into the future. He says it's because we don't care about ourselves in the future, which could be one reason why many people don't invest in pensions. Perhaps it's because we have no template to apply, unless there's a strong family likeness throughout. Otherwise, it seems that old age is a foreign country to us – you know you'll go there some time, but until your boat starts rocking in the tides around its shore you won't turn your mind to it. Recently I asked a group of experienced counsellors to describe how they see themselves in old age, and not one of them could do it. We simply can't picture ourselves as old, which makes me smile because I know many seniors who don't see themselves as being old, either!

There may be other factors, although they would affect fewer people. If we have had a bad personal experience of an older person, say an unkind or manipulative older relative, we might subconsciously transfer those negative emotions to other people we meet. This kind of transference is observed in other contexts where it can result in generalized labelling of a whole group or race, such as "IT people are monosyllabic (or grunt)", "Scottish people are dour", or "Blondes are not academic", and so on.

How ageism works

Charity Age UK says that ageist attitudes can negatively affect someone's confidence, job prospects, financial situation, and quality of life. Ageism can also include the way that older people are represented in the media, which can have a wider impact on the public's attitudes.

Ageism subjects older people to discriminatory practices, for instance in employment, as already mentioned, and in services. It makes them the subject of jokes that would not be tolerated if they were directed at ethnic groups or the other sex. For example, comedians and talk show hosts joke about seniors and memory loss; doctors often talk past a senior patient to an adult child as if the senior wasn't even in the room; younger adults mock seniors for being "slow"; and commercial advertisements depict seniors as out of date and lacking knowledge about modern culture and new technologies. I often have BBC Radio 4 murmuring in the background and turn it up if something interesting comes on, but had it not been an expensive Bose® system I would have stamped on it the morning I heard a comedian tell a joke about older women not knowing the difference between iPads and TENA® pads, a type of incontinence pad. Would he have been allowed to make the same joke about Black or Asian women? At the moment, people can make as many similar jokes about older people as they like with impunity.

Ageist discrimination in services

The perception of older drivers is that they are doddery, slow, and uncertain. But research published in 2016 showed that, contrary to most people's understanding, older people are safer drivers than younger ones. Analysis of data on vehicle accidents showed that drivers aged 70 are involved in three to four times fewer accidents than 17- to 21-year-old men. Young men are more likely to be involved in incidents resulting from driving too fast and losing control. The study found that most mistakes made by older people occurred during right turns and overtaking, and when they felt under pressure from other drivers.

Yet premiums for older people have been rising at a faster pace than for any other age group. The number of drivers aged 70 and older is rising by 10,000 a month. There are now more than a million drivers in the UK in their 80s, an advisor suggested, and this older population of drivers is turning into a nice little earner for insurance firms in the UK. "Unjustified age discrimination is illegal in most other parts of day-to-day life in Britain. It should be illegal in the insurance industry too," said Caroline Abrahams of Age UK, the charity and lobby group.

A national newspaper has been bombarded with complaints about two insurance companies that advertise themselves as representing the needs of older customers, but which have routinely hiked premiums when contracts have been due for renewal. In one instance, a policy premium rose by 25 per cent at renewal — only for the firm later to promise to match an identical quote offered by a rival. English actress Sheila Hancock wrote to the BBC's *Money Programme* when her motor insurance was increased from £873 a year to £2,246 once she passed her 80th birthday, despite her not having made a claim for years. Another press report said it is commonplace and should be outlawed.

In hospitals, older patients are sometimes treated by staff as though they were children. This particularly distressed the daughter whose father was "highly intelligent, unfailingly courteous, reserved, and dignified". Towards the end of his life nobody seemed interested in what he used to be (or, as I would put it, who he really was), and addressed him as "dear" or "darling", or as part of the ubiquitous "we". "He hated it. I hated it," she wrote in a letter to a newspaper. But I need to add that it's not true of all nurses. An elderly relative of mine spent months in hospital last year and was treated with the greatest respect.

In an episode of the BBC's *You and Yours* radio programme, presenter Winifred Robinson listened for the best part of an hour to people aged between 70 and 100-plus calling in to say how they liked to be treated and addressed. Most of them insisted they did not want to be patronized, or called "dear", or by their first name, unless they'd been asked and given permission. They insisted that they wanted to be seen as themselves, not as a stereotypical older person. Typical was a woman who said, with superb diction, "I am 95, and I want to be addressed as an equal."

Ageism moulds our expectations

Dr Butler tells of the man who was a participant in a long-term research study. He'd turned 101 when he went to his physician to ask advice about a painful knee. "What do you expect at your age?" he was asked. To this typical statement by a physician, Mr Rocklin replied indignantly, "So why doesn't my left leg hurt?" The symmetry of the human body offers a good test of the realities of medical ageism, says Dr Butler, and Rocklin's oft-quoted response has been used by many geriatricians to educate medical students.

Dr Butler noted that, in social scientist George Mead's "looking-glass self" concept, "older people may turn ageist prejudice inward, absorbing, accepting, and identifying with the discrimination". Identifying with the discrimination means accepting it as true and believing it of yourself. It is a corrosion of God's design for life because He made us social beings that develop in relationship with one another and, as mentioned earlier, our view of ourselves is hugely influenced by what is reflected to us by others. An empty-mirror syndrome is a telling description of a condition sometimes suffered by children who grow up lacking a sense of identity because of poor nurturing in their early years.

"The Invisible Gorilla"

When group identity is devalued, as in the case of seniors, individuals actively engage in dissociating themselves from the devalued group. That dissociation can be so deep that it can lead to not just discounting people in the group, but not seeing them at all.

There's an experiment that is one of the best known in psychology, called "The Invisible Gorilla".[17] To demonstrate a trait known as Selective Attention, students were asked to watch a short video in which six people, three wearing white shirts and three wearing black, pass basketballs to each other. The watching students were to keep a silent count of the number of passes made by the people in white shirts. A few minutes into the exercise, as the six people were passing the ball one to another, a large person dressed in a gorilla suit strolled into the middle of the action, faced the camera, thumped its chest, and then left, spending nine seconds on screen. That would interrupt the count, you might think! But half of the people who watched the video and counted the passes failed to see the gorilla. It was as though he had been invisible. They were so focused on the players in white passing the ball that they did not see him at all.

It explains how, with our minds accepting the magnification of adulthood, we fail to see the gorilla of ageism. Our brains have a marvellous way of screening out anything that we have decided is not relevant to us. Neurologist Suzanne O'Sullivan remembers the first time she saw the invisible gorilla experiment shown at a conference.

"I did not see the gorilla. My mind had simply discarded it. What amazed me was that I had not blocked out something meaningless and trivial, only paying attention to the thing that interested me. I had seen the trivial and instead discarded something so flagrant and incongruous that it was a struggle for me to believe it had ever really been there."[18]

Selective attention is one of the reasons older people find themselves invisible. Some tell us with very little prompting that that's how they find they have become. "Why do people become invisible as they get old?" asked a psychology website (Quora). None of the respondents had a satisfactory answer, but there were a couple of interesting observations, including one that mentions a Harry Potter style "cloak of invisibility" story. It was about a woman who loved watching films at her local Cineplex, a multi-studio cinema. Her friend posted, "She'd go to the Cineplex and, feeling assured that a 16-year-old usher couldn't even distinguish what she looked like (an old lady, with grey hair and glasses), she would finish up one movie and go to another without paying. She was seen any number of times, and yet no one asked her what she was doing." The person posting added, "Why not use the cunning that being alive for so long has earned you?"

Another post told about helping "a little lady who was stumbling around a hospital parking lot trying to find her car, a bright red sporty Z28 Camaro. I asked if it was her car or her grandson's. She replied that it was hers, and she needed a young person's car or no one would notice her."

Anthropologist Barbara Myerhoff wrote about "death by invisibility" when she described an older woman, an "unseen" pedestrian on a sidewalk, who was killed by a cyclist.[19] Invisibility was also seen after the World Trade Center attack in New York in September 2011 when, within 24 hours, animal activists evacuated dogs and cats while disabled and older people were abandoned in their apartments for up to seven days before ad hoc medical teams arrived to rescue them.[20]

Older people were also largely invisible in the news reporting of the devastation caused by Hurricane Katrina in New Orleans, except for a moving story about two adult grandsons who forcibly, but with great affection, removed their grandfather from the upper floor of the flooded family home he'd built himself and refused to leave to the mercy of the looters. Once safely in the boat, slung over his grandson's shoulder, the elderly man told the cameraman that he was only going because they were bigger than he was. "He's kind of ornery, ain't he?" said one grandson, with a grin.

Apart from one or two reports, older people are not mentioned in the current conflict in the Middle East. Mention in the media of older people is so sparse that I asked a Christian Aid agency active in the region if they had any stories of older people to share. What was happening to them? Were they escaping, and, if not, how were they surviving? The agency had no stories, despite their embeddedness, but said they would investigate. After a while they said couldn't find any. There were a few pictures of adults fleeing from a war zone carrying their parents and elderly relatives with them, and one of a man who carried a frail elderly lady for something like 100 miles, but these stories were few and far between.

An encouraging note here is that when people do see what's happening to someone in the "invisible generation", they can be overwhelmingly kind. A retired teacher, aged 87, wrote a poignant open letter to a national newspaper saying that since her husband had died six months previously she had felt increasingly "invisible" in her community. "No one wants you when you're old," she said. Her neighbours never called on her. "It was different when we came here... my husband and myself (sic) looked after old and elderly neighbours. We did have help from a couple about three years ago, but since then nothing." Within hours of the newspaper highlighting her plight, she was inundated with offers of help and companionship from neighbours, schoolchildren, and others.

Ageism in the media

For a couple of years I wrote a regular column for a well-known Christian magazine. The editor knew my work and had invited me to send in a regular contribution about issues concerning old age. The stories I supplied were usually "hard" news stories. They included the story of a Japanese pensioner who had committed suicide by self-immolation because he feared he didn't have enough money to survive, and there was quite a big story of a parliamentary review that had exposed the way tens of thousands of frail older people (yes, *tens* of thousands) had been unlawfully taken from their homes into residential care by council social workers, who seized their assets and, in some cases, even sold their homes to pay for it. In one case, a Court of Protection judge said a 93-year-old had been spared years of misery, because his friend had complained persistently and effectively. The judge commended the friend, and ordered the council to pay financial recompense to the 93-year-old, return him to his own home, and care for him free of charge until his death. The story highlighted the importance of being a friend to the elderly.

To end on an upbeat note for my last column, I sent in a little article under the title "Mature Members Helping Churches Grow". More and more seniors are involved in outreach programmes, and membership is rising as a result. But when it was published the title had been altered to "Oldies Growing Church". When I complained to the editor, he said that he was sorry, but not everyone objects to the word "oldies". Because this is my "thing" and I wanted to be sure I wasn't over-reacting, I ran it on my social media pages. Responses were quick and definite, saying that it was demeaning, disparaging, and dismissive. One observed that "you wouldn't use a derogatory term like that with an ethnic group".

But this is mild compared with secular media, which are perhaps the biggest drivers of ageism as they have such a widespread impact on the public's attitude. Some of the starkest examples surfaced in the months leading up to the European Union referendum in 2016. Polls had shown that older people were more likely to vote to leave the EU than younger people and pro-EU commentators were saying, quite openly, that it was because older people were too stupid to see the advantages of remaining in the Union. It caused quite a flurry on social media, with an infuriated 34-year-old leave voter writing that she was neither old nor uneducated, but a hard-working university lecturer. Similar postings and letters to the press included an offshore helicopter pilot writing that his wife was a surgeon and his mother-in-law a former president of a prestigious medical association, and they had all voted to leave.

The argument raged on, with others asserting that the older generation had taken the best of the good economic times and were now tossing the young to their fate by voting to leave. No one, as far as I know, examined the reasons why older people, with their longer life experience, wanted to leave the EU. After the referendum the volume increased. Just for the record, data released after the vote revealed that 40 per cent of those aged 65 or over, and 43 per cent of 55- to 64-year-olds, voted to remain.

The men's magazine *GQ* said outright, "We should ban old people from voting." For good measure, it added that those of retirement age have little or no stake in the country's next era. They will all die before it comes in, it implied. Clearly, *GQ* editors hadn't read the statistics about lengthening lifespans.

A cartoon in a newspaper captured the mood eloquently. The drawing was of younger people propelling older people in wheelchairs to the edge of a cliff and tipping them over. No caption was needed: the picture said it all.

In the *Financial Times*, in an article entitled "Cull the Grey Vote", journalist Jeremy Paxman argued that older people should not be allowed to vote in the referendum because they "scarcely know what day of the week it is, yet their ballot papers are worth the same as a Cambridge professor's. And politicians know that older people are much more likely to vote – as one put it to me privately, 'There's not much else going on in lots of their lives.'" He added that the young are concerned about many things, whereas "Old people simply moulder away in their bungalows, watching them increase in value".

Some commentators suggested that Mr Paxman should get out more, especially as he is now entitled to a free bus pass since he's reached the age of 67. He should meet people like naturalist and film-maker David Attenborough, now over 90 and still producing excellent work. And I wonder what he would say if introduced to Queen Elizabeth, who celebrated her 90th birthday the same year as David Attenborough. He might also like to talk to the lively nonagenarians who took part in ITV's celebration of the Queen's 90th birthday. They included Judith Kerr, the illustrator and writer of children's books such as *The Tiger Who Came To Tea*; two of her new books were released in 2015. And Jean Miller, a Vidal Sassoon hairdresser who drives an hour to work and an hour back each day. Also fashion designer Joan Burstein, still working at her Bond Street store. There are many more. I have a file so full of stories of people like this I've stopped collecting them: they're becoming the norm.

Yet they're reported in the media as exceptions. But seeing them as exceptions is a form of benevolent ageism according to Thomas Scharf, Professor of Social Gerontology at Newcastle University. "It makes the very much older person who is active seem a breed apart, but they are only older versions of us."[21] "Older versions of us" is a concept as far as the sun is from the moon for younger adults who took part in the Princeton study. The researchers said their attitude was worrying because the young people will eventually grow old themselves and become part of the "targeted demographic".

"Targeted" is a good verb in this context. Seniors are being targeted as responsible for many of the woes of the younger generation. They should move aside from high-paying jobs and prominent social roles to make way for younger people, and they are seen as consuming too many scarce resources, such as health care. This ageist stereotyping could become even darker as the number of seniors grows, says Princeton University psychological scientist Susan Fiske. It will become more hostile and will be wielded mostly by the young in an acrimonious generational conflict. We look at this in more detail in Chapter 4.

Ageism can be life-threatening

In 2014, a report by the charity Macmillan Cancer Support revealed that an estimated 14,000 people over the age of 75 were denied cancer treatment by "ageist" consultants.[22] In May 2015 a group of specialists on ageing wrote to *The Lancet* challenging the framework of a UN directive which they said sent out the message that health provision for younger groups must be prioritized at the expense of older people. In 2015, research by Professor Raphael Cohen-Almagor of the University of Hull revealed that thousands of elderly patients in Belgian hospitals had been euthanized by their doctors without their or their families' consent. Decisions to euthanize were based solely on the doctors' subjective view of their patient's quality of life. At the same time there were reports of older people in Holland carrying "Do Not Euthanize" cards in their pockets, in case they were suddenly taken ill.

At the time of writing, funding for adult social care in the UK has been cut by 36 per cent over the last five years, despite the increasing number of older people and warnings of the danger posed to the elderly. Last year saw the biggest rise in deaths of people aged 65 and over, particularly among 80-year-olds and mostly of elderly women. Life expectancy was rising for this age group until 2013; instead of being a positive figure of an additional six years 40 weeks for a woman aged 85, it's now a negative figure of minus ten weeks.

Last year's death figures were the highest for 50 years. Data from the Office of National Statistics showed that there were 5.4 per cent more deaths in England – equating to almost 27,000 extra deaths, prompting warnings by Public Health England (PHE) of an urgent crisis in the care of the elderly. Public health advisors said the elderly were now bearing the brunt of a growing crisis in the NHS and cuts to social care, with women suffering the most. Professor Danny Dorling of Oxford University, an expert on older-age life expectancy, said, "When we look at

2015, we are not just looking at one bad year. We have seen excessive mortality – especially among women – since 2012. I suspect the largest factor here is cuts to social services – to meals on wheels, to visits to the elderly." Age UK has been warning for some time that around a million older people are unable to obtain funding for care, and are facing "catastrophe". How can one of the world's most advanced societies allow old people to die simply because of lack of care?[23] Recently a government spokesman said that people should care for their older parents as they do for their children, but, quite apart from the moral and practical questions this would raise, commentators were swift to point out that many older people simply do not have children or families.

Time to put their light on a stand

"No one lights a lamp and then puts it under a basket. Instead, a lamp is placed on a stand, where it gives light to everyone in the house," says Matthew 5:15. Ageism is something of the shadows, spurred by myths based on misperceptions and ignorance of the facts. Today's seniors are helping to support their adult children, contributing to their communities, and boosting the national Exchequer by billions of pounds each year. Many charities would collapse without their voluntary work – which in itself is worth billions a year. As the RVS report mentioned, they are the glue that holds society together and life would be more dangerous without them. And, in frail old age, when ageism would have them wheeled to the cliff and tipped over, their prayers are heard in heaven and are influencing events in a way we'll never fully understand here on earth. It's time to let these facts be known – time to put their lamp on a stand. We are instructed to expose the "works of darkness" (Ephesians 5:11) and we do that by exposing them to the light.

* * * *

This has been a long chapter, and examining ageism can be depressing. It's a bit like walking through a muddy field that is heavy going. We need to remind ourselves that, although our outer body is decaying, our inner being is being renewed by Him, day by day (2 Corinthians 4:16). And that the real us – the real "me", planned in advance and designed by God Himself – is not the one we see now.

We'll all be called Home at some point. But until then there is debris to be swept away and airspace to be cleared. God wants His seniors to recognize their value and take their places in a restored elderhood, reflecting His values – and His works – to all generations. Recently, a publisher sent me a copy of a book published two years ago, written by 100-year-old Douglas Higgins.[24] It's a fascinating autobiography. The letter writers, Ian and Jean Murray, said that Douglas was still living in his own house and they had no doubt he would be happy to talk to me. They gave me his landline number so I telephoned, leaving a message on the answerphone. Douglas called back more or less straight away, and we had a lively conversation lasting for about 15 minutes. He is one of the few people I've met who talk as much and as fast as I do: so much for inevitable slowdown in old age, I thought. Even so, at 102 he is not as strong as he used to be. He said, "I now pray and ask the Lord now that I'm unable to speak [publicly] or preach, will He use my book and my testimony in His mercy and grace to call others to Himself?"

Then he added, "It has occurred! A pupil of mine that I taught in 1947 got my book, read it, and came to know the Lord Jesus Christ!"

Douglas and his book are an example of elderhood in action. And in encouraging him and enabling the publication, Ian and Jean Murray exemplify the type of support we can be giving our seniors so they are able to fulfil the role God has designed for them.

Chapter 4
Fighting the Invisible Gorilla

My eyes popped at a paragraph in an invitation to a conference at a well-known northern university on the future of ageing. It read, "Since 2007, the real disposable income of pensioners has risen by almost 10 per cent. Those over the age of 65 have harvested fully two-thirds of that £2.7tn increase in national wealth." In a few words, it painted a picture of today's pensioners as a bunch of wealthy retired pirates, living in luxury.

Of course, it's far from the truth. It was written by an economist, and economists generally don't seem to like older people. One wrote an article saying that they slow down global growth, because they don't purchase as much as those who are younger. This should make us ask – *what kind of society have we built that we value a person by their spending power?* But the economist's statement was a broad brush stroke that covered over a multitude of contrasting facts, one of which is that around a million older people in the UK are living in real poverty (Age UK, 2016). And that, as in the general population, something like 10 per cent of people in the older generation have 90 per cent of the wealth.

The invitation came alongside a stream of media reports blaming the older generation for the economic woes that younger adults are struggling with. Themes such as "older people have saddled the younger generation with an excessive bill for state pensions, while grabbing an ever-greater share of

NHS spending," and "Generation Y Betrayed". But the truth about the older generation is that, far from being a burden and a drain, in the UK pensioners make a net contribution of £44 billion a year to the Exchequer. That is a *net contribution*: after deducting costs for health, social care, and pensions. And it's expected to rise to £75 billion by 2030. These figures, and more, are contained in a report published by the RVS of a study conducted by leading economic and social consultants SQW.

Intergenerational war

These "blame" statements are part of an intergenerational war that wants government to remove benefits from the older generation to give them to the younger. And there's no denying that it's tough on millennials: employment and housing are huge problems. But were these conditions caused by older people? They were not: they were caused by globalization and the "Great Recession", as the 2008 banking crash is now being called. In an extraordinary talk at Liverpool John Moores University in early December 2016, the Governor of the Bank of England, Mark Carney, warned that globalization had not "raised everybody's boat" and that many people had paid "a heavy price" and had come to associate it with low wages, insecure employment, stateless corporations, and "striking inequalities". He said, "Many citizens in advanced economies are facing heightened uncertainty, lamenting a loss of control and losing trust in the system. To them, measures of aggregate progress bear little relation to their own experience."

Anxieties had been made worse by the "twin crises of solvency and integrity at the heart of finance. When the financial crisis hit, the world's largest banks were shown to be operating in a 'heads-I-win-tails-you-lose' bubble: widespread rigging of some core markets was exposed, and masters of the universe became minions. Few in positions of power accepted responsibility, and shareholders, taxpayers and citizens paid the heavy price".[25]

Millennials are feeling the backwash of the 2008 financial crash and the results of globalization, in which today's pensioners had no part – the "masters of the universe" were generally under the age of 50. It's true that today's pensioners experienced years of steady employment, and were able to retire on generous defined-benefit pension plans and "got to cash out their home and retirement assets before the 2008 crash",[26] but they had been the beneficiaries of years of benign circumstances, not pirates who stole it all away. The crash also badly affected pensioners. They are still losing after pension funds plummeted, affecting pay-outs, and they've also lost the value of their savings over the last few years, as these are currently paying almost zero interest rates.

Many seniors are writing to the press to put the record straight. "I left school at 15 and worked until 65," wrote one; "during those 50 years I paid full National Insurance, as did every employer that I worked for. In some years it was in excess of 23 per cent [of salary]; therefore my state pension, which people would struggle to live on, is not a 'benefit' or a 'handout'; it is a well-earned entitlement."

Replying to an argument that presented the welfare budget as a two-way conflict between favoured pensioners and the low-paid below retirement age, another writer pointed out that absolute commercialism has turned morality on its head, since those who have saved and contributed towards creating a degree of security for themselves after retirement are seen as depriving low-paid workers and the disabled of the benefits required to top up their incomes to the level that will sustain life. "The true beneficiaries... are not the pensioners," he concludes, "but the shareholders whose companies refuse to pay a wage sufficient for the maintenance of a family home."

"We did not have it all, and that we should give away what we have to the new generation is a misconception that is gaining ground," wrote a woman from Hampshire. Her generation had grown up with rationing, even of power supplies. About 95 per cent went to work at 15. Yes, there were no university fees, but, with few places, most were unable to go. Only 13 per cent of people aged 65 to 69 have a university degree, and bright girls were often told that a university education wasn't an option, because they'd only get married anyway. Careers were often limited by prejudice and sexism. Many began married life renting rooms in other people's homes. "We bought dilapidated houses and spent time and energy doing them up. We had furniture passed down through the family, and two-thirds of our income went on the mortgage – interest rates were high; there was little left for treats like going away on holiday. Our cars were mainly old bangers, a meal out was a rare treat, convenience foods were unheard of, and new clothes were rare: many of us sewed or knitted our own. Now we keep the economy going by providing free childcare after school, during holidays, and on training days. And, finally, the chances are that we shall need any assets we've accrued to spend on expensive nursing care."

Cari Rosen and Rowan Davies, editors of Gransnet, the social networking site for Britain's 14 million grandparents, say that bashing the older generation has become a new form of bigotry. They say that the younger generation, "weighed down with student debt and struggling to get on the housing ladder, are accusing older people, sitting complacently in mortgage-free family homes and living comfortably off index-linked pensions, of causing their pain." Gransnet research confirms that the older generation generally did have a better quality of life than any other generation, but that many of them are hurt and irritated by wild assumptions about their lifestyles. "We seem to be described as sitting in huge houses we should vacate for younger people, as 'wealthy pensioners', 'bed blockers', 'greedy'," spluttered one pensioner, aghast at how ageism is the one form of bigotry that is cheerfully tolerated.[27]

"I am one offended baby boomer," wrote a 68-year-old to a Christian magazine.[28] She was responding to an article that had blamed environmental damage on her generation. "Not so," she replied. "We washed nappies and didn't buy disposables that do not biodegrade easily, as parents do today. We rinsed and returned milk and fizzy drink bottles. As for recycling, we had one small, lidded trash can, and paper was given to the salvage man. In the 1970s, geography lessons included caring for the environment."

On a different topic, one that highlights the contrast in attitudes, she wrote that some things are more difficult now for the young. "Immorality is the norm and you are seen as weird if you try to not have sex before marriage… Everyone who expects to trust their spouse and have a stable and happily family life is stupid, as far as magazines and the media are concerned. But that is a different subject." It's true, it is a different subject, but it highlights the vast gap between the culture that we have now and the way it was then.

Nastier ageism

In 2013, as the recession gripped, Princeton University psychological scientist Susan Fiske predicted the emergence of a new and nastier ageism that would "likely be more hostile than what we've known so far, and what's more, it will be wielded mostly by the young in an acrimonious generational conflict". When older people work for longer and do not retire, the younger see them as limiting their job opportunities. In many ways, the younger see their "entitlements" being eroded by the older, particularly when resources are under pressure, such as health and social benefits. "They expect ageing Boomers to cede... scarce resources to the young."[29] Why do they do this? Along with others, Fiske observes that, "Young people are motivated to draw and enforce generational boundaries for the sake of their own self-esteem and autonomy."

Understanding what drives intergenerational warfare – the myths and negative thinking – makes it easier to challenge. We would rather that unpleasantness like this just went away quietly and didn't bother us at all, but it's here and it's being robustly promoted. An organization dedicated to sponsoring it, with a view to influencing government decisions so that they are "fair" to young adults, states on its website that it is looking for people who will take their cause into schools, to speak to students. We are told to "take no part in the worthless deeds of evil and darkness; instead, expose them" (Ephesians 5:11). Wherever we come across it, we have to speak out and say, no, that's not right.

Recognizing and challenging this "nastier ageism" is important because (as mentioned in Chapter 1) God planned life so that we would develop in relationship with others. Our core beliefs about ourselves and our values are formed in response to the way others treat us. It's as true of older people as it is of children. The findings of a recent American study showed that older people who have been conditioned to think they are physically and mentally decrepit in old age are stressed by negative thoughts that can actually alter the structure of the brain and trigger dementia.[30] Professor Tom Kitwood (in *Dementia Reconsidered*) wrote that every event is a neurological event, creating either a benign biochemical environment conducive to neuronal health – or the opposite. Yale psychologist Becca R. Levy found that a constant bombardment of negative stereotypes increased blood pressure. Depression and stress both increase the risk of dementia by nearly 50 per cent. Clearly, taking on board negative thoughts to the extent that they can alter the structure of the brain can be as dangerous as birds flying into the engines of Captain Sully's plane in Manhattan in 2009.

Even some lyrics in songs that show old age in a negative way could harm the health of the elderly, researchers at Hull and Anglia Ruskin Universities have found. An example they quoted was the Beatles' "When I'm Sixty-Four", written by Paul McCartney when he was 15. References to getting older, losing one's hair, and questioning whether the romance of receiving a valentine will continue associate old age with being unlovable, researchers said. They found that three-quarters of the 76 popular songs written since 1930 that focus on ageing showed old age in a bad light, with pensioners portrayed as frail or pitiful.

So how can you prevent ageist thoughts from flying into your mind? Not by smacking your hand on your forehead and declaring that you will have no part in these ageist prejudices, to paraphrase a comment in an article in *The Times* by Irish journalist Terry Prone. Commenting on a leaflet he'd received in the post, proclaiming "Say No to Ageism", he said, "No doubt its backers hope that someone who is deeply prejudiced when it comes to older people will stop in front of this poster, take a look at the nice, crumpled, granny face in the picture, smack a hand to their forehead and promise to change their ways, making a firm purpose of amendment to henceforth promulgate the contribution to society made by older people." No, he insisted, it will take more than that. Only changing the law will change behaviour, as it did with motorists and wearing seat belts. He declared, "Ageism, like racism and sexism, is based on an assumption that one group in society is… less worthwhile than everybody else, *thus permitting the rest of us to amputate their rights*"[31] (my italics). "Don't preach to us about ageism," he insists; "change the law."

Keeping the airspace free

I wondered what tactics airports use to keep their airspace free from birds and whether they could be metaphors that we could learn from. Interestingly, the first one isn't even metaphorical.

"You just need vigilance – continuous monitoring, continuous adaptation of your mitigation techniques. It's not anything that will ever be completely eliminated," says Christopher Oswald, vice-president for safety and technical operations for Airports Council International – North America.[32] It's a management issue rather than a problem that will ever be solved. The first tip, then, is to be vigilant. Do some meta-thinking: when thinking about older people or the ageing process, or any issues of old age, take a helicopter view of your mind and watch what you are thinking. Feelings can be so strong, and assumptions so ingrained, that they can be mistaken for facts. A theme in cognitive behavioural therapy (CBT) is to look for the evidence that supports a negative thought – and there is usually none.

The second is to clear away conditions that attract them. "If you don't have the attraction, the wildlife is not going to be there," Oswald says. Scientists are experimenting with planting grasses at airports that Canada geese don't like to eat, as well as laying gravel to replace grassy areas between runways. Removing ponds and trees that bear fruit or seeds is another way of discouraging birds.

Do we have in our minds something like airports' grassy spaces? Preconceptions that would attract ageist thinking, or make us susceptible to it? Could we have unconsciously absorbed secular values, and formed hidden schemas that act like airport ponds and grassy places, so that ageist views have a place to land on in us? One of the most telling of Jesus' phrases after He had told His disciples that He wouldn't be talking with them much more because the "prince of this world" was coming, was that he had no power over Him because "he hath nothing in me" (John 14:30). There was no landing place for Satan in Jesus. In Psalm 139 King David wrote, "Search me, O God, and know my heart: try me, and know my thoughts: And see if there be any wicked way in me, and lead me in the way everlasting."

Negative schemas remain dormant until they're triggered. If you're not sure about this, ask yourself what value seniors would bring to your church, or to your workplace, or even to your life. You may find yourself reflexively thinking, as did my 50-something friend, that they have nothing of value to bring. If you do – you have a grassy landing place. It's also a breeding ground for thoughts that will affect not just how you see older people, but how you see yourself in old age. In airport parlance, it's a "breeding ground for the prey base, particularly the rodents that attract large-body raptors." Salt Lake City Airport's wildlife manager, Gib Rokich, says, "It goes all the way down to midges to grasshoppers to army worms."[33] As the Scripture says, "It's the little foxes that spoil the vineyard" (Song of Solomon 2:15).

Pyrotechnics are a common tool for scaring birds away with noise, according to airport managers. "Shell crackers" are fireworks blasted hundreds of feet away by a shotgun. Smaller "bangers" can be shot from a starter's pistol. "Screamers" sound like bottle rockets fired from a pistol. The disadvantage of these methods is that an employee has to go out near the birds and fire off the noises, making it labour-intensive and costly. It sounds like a job for small boys and teenagers.

Could we compare these tactics to the noise we can make by our speaking out and firing shots against ageism each time we see it? At my church house group a woman in her 70s took her mobile (cell) phone to a store because the charger had stopped working. It wasn't the fuse because she'd checked that. The store assistant noted that it was rather an old phone now, all of ten years old, and wouldn't it be a good idea to upgrade it? But the 70-something had insisted on this particular phone at the time and had kept it because she didn't want all the bells and whistles that come with the others. "I want to phone, and to text," she insisted; "that's all. A phone should be for messages, not for Kindles or navigating through town or even for the new 'windingey' Bible studies our church is using." (She bought the book instead – though the software is excellent!) On the other hand, she is an avid internet user, searching for information, using spreadsheets, and sending emails. The assistant told her that she couldn't match a new charger with this old phone but that it could probably be found on the internet, and perhaps a relative could look it up for her? "The implication was that I wasn't up to using a computer," said my indignant house-group mate. She didn't say anything; she simply left the store, but the rest of us were quick to suggest suitable retorts that were the equivalent of the small "bangers" from a starter's pistol.

Journalist Terry Prone's piece in *The Times* could be compared to a shell cracker. Your letters to your local press and emails to your Member of Parliament or Congressman are the same. Perhaps a "screamer" would be questions asked in parliament, or a statement by a very prominent person, and reported widely in the media, though the introduction of a law would be the best.

Another airport tactic is to use dogs and falcons. Sky is a border collie, the third dog to patrol Southwest Florida International Airport in Fort Myers since 1999. "The dog is a natural predator – they never get used to her," says James Hess, airside operations supervisor for the airport. Sky works seven days a week, running into foliage too dense for vehicles and across wetlands that slow people down. She isn't out to catch the birds, just to scatter them away from the runways. "I don't want to go into water waist-deep myself, or even ankle-deep, for that matter," Hess says. "She can definitely get into areas that we cannot." We can be "border collies" for others, watching out for them and keeping negative thoughts away with a steady stream of positive encouragement. It's where our church fellowships are so valuable.

Spiritual weapons for spiritual warfare

We can't use dogs to combat ageism – but a powerful weapon we do have is prayer. Prayer can go into areas that we can't. Prayer can change attitudes and mindsets, or, to be more accurate, the Holy Spirit can do these things in response to our prayers. "The king's heart is a stream of water in the hand of the Lord; he turns it wherever he will," says Proverbs 21:1 (ESV). We can pray that ageism will be made illegal, for example. We can pray that it will be seen for what it is; not just mildly deprecating humour but damaging bigotry.

Ageism is so diametrically opposed to God's purposes for His older people that its origin is self-evident. Writing to the Christians at Ephesus, the apostle Paul pointed directly to the satanic root of their struggles, saying that they were "not fighting against flesh-and-blood enemies, but against evil rulers and authorities of the unseen world, against mighty powers in this dark world, and against evil spirits in the heavenly places".

Satan does not want God's seniors to "tell of His goodness", or to be all that God intends them to be. The enemy of our souls does not want "elderhood"; he wants passive, disengaged, self-protective seniors who are disempowered by the low view they have of themselves. Ageism is a strategy of the devil, and Paul tells the Ephesians to put on their spiritual armour, so they will be able to stand against him (Ephesians 6:15–17). "In addition to all of these, hold up the shield of faith to stop the fiery arrows of the devil. Put on salvation as your helmet, and take the sword of the Spirit, which is the word of God" (NLT).

Of course, it isn't true that all young adults are against older people. We meet people at our conferences and events who don't regard them as "other", and even have a special affection for them. From time to time Christian radio stations will call me for a comment on an item that is in the news, and the producer and I will chat before and after the interview has been recorded or aired. Transworld Radio UK (TWR UK) is one of them, and although I've spoken with quite a few of their producers, the two I remember best are James and Hannah. James is one of those young adults who like people of all ages. And Hannah, who's in her 20s, told me that when it came to choosing a church house group to belong to after moving to a new district and a new church, she chose the one that had the most older people. "They're much more interesting than people my age," she said; "they want to listen to you, and they'll pray for you. They have had so many experiences, and they have really interesting stories!"

At a national gathering a girl in her early 20s came to our stand and asked if we (my colleague and I on the stand) thought she would be suitable for work in one of our Pilgrim Homes. "Would I have a chance?" she asked. She was working with children but had always wanted to work with older people, and hadn't seen an opportunity until now. We said that her very wanting to do it was a good sign that God was calling her and assured her that every Pilgrim Home has first-class assessment and training programmes, and gave her contact details. She was so delighted I think she almost skipped down the aisle away from us.

We shouldn't ignore ageism: we do need to take a stand against it (Ephesians 5:11). We have a role that God has predestined us to fill, and we must demolish anything that stands in the way. Anything that warps our expectations of our future has to be destroyed. Not far from where I live, in South Wales, are examples of why this is so important.

Living scars

If you're not familiar with British history, particularly the Welsh side of it, you may not have heard of Aneurin ("Nye") Bevan. We'd find that hard to believe in this part of Wales, because here he's something of a hero. Things are named after him, including the local health trust. As Minister for Health in the Labour Government in 1948, he steered the National Health Service into being. He fervently believed that medical treatment and health care should be available to everyone, regardless of their ability to pay. Nye was the son of a South Wales coal miner, and he'd worked in the local mine himself. It wasn't just the custom for sons to follow their fathers in this way – there was hardly any other source of employment. Entire communities, whole families, depended on the local mine.

The conditions they worked in were unbelievably brutal. Just north of Pontypool is the tiny town of Blaenavon, now a World Heritage Site, which has an industrial heritage museum centred on a closed colliery called the Big Pit. It's staffed by former miners, and offers "a unique underground tour of a real coalmine, where hundreds of men, women and children once worked to extract the precious mineral that stoked furnaces and lit the household fires of the world". Yes – women and children.[34] (In the Victorian era, the thing that offended polite society most was not the minimal clothing of the women working in the underground heat, but the fact that they wore trousers.) Also down the pit are the stalls where the pit donkeys lived, except for two weeks of the year in the holiday break when they were brought up to the surface, their eyes shielded from the daylight. You're also shown the spot where children, some as young as six years old, would sit opening and closing doors to provide ventilation.

I once went down the Big Pit and felt it must have been the nearest thing to visiting hell. The walls glistened with black coal and without the modern electric lighting it was dark and bleak. "The sound of rushing water you can hear is in the big pipes bringing it down the mountain," said the guide, "but in the old days it wasn't in pipes; it was just left to run down through the mine and the men had to work in it. A lot suffered with rheumatism and arthritis." That wasn't all. A report published in 2008 noted that "even to this day, there is a legacy of ill health that may be traced to the patterns of heavy and extractive industries established... during the industrial revolution".[35] They certainly extracted the health of the miners, inflicting numerous diseases, including "black lung disease" (pneumoconiosis), crippled legs, curvature of the spine, skin irritations, heart disease, ruptures, asthma, bronchitis, and rheumatism. Sometimes accidents in the mines took their lives too, with roof collapses and gas explosions, suffocation, and gas poisoning. It was a horrible way to earn a living.

But, despite the inhuman conditions, at the height of the industry the colliers did not become brutalized. Underground, looking out for each other's safety, and there was a camaraderie that blessed their souls. Above ground there were lively valley chapels that lifted their spirits. Singing used to be as natural as breathing in Wales, especially hymns and arias. Families were close and communities real.

When the mines closed, the economy of entire regions collapsed. It was catastrophic. Tens of thousands of families were rescued by the state welfare safety net, and went onto "benefits". It took a long time to attract other employers to the valleys, although the Welsh Development Agency did its best, but there are still areas with families in which three or four generations have grown up not knowing what it is to be employed, or even to be employable.

A few years ago a large company announced plans to move into one of these areas, with something like 15,000 jobs on offer. The company advertised and promoted itself vigorously, advertising in local press and "job shops", and holding open days in public places. Instead of an avalanche of job seekers, they had barely a trickle. National television moved in when the story came out that applications had been received for less than 10 per cent of the jobs. A commentator explained that it wasn't because people were especially lazy or had become dependent on state handouts, but that they were held back by low self-worth and a lack of confidence in their abilities. Their expectations of what they can do have been ground down by their perceived lack of worth.

This was something that the tireless Aneurin Bevan, who never lost his passion for the people of South Wales, had dreaded. He once said that his greatest fear was that when new horizons opened and possibilities presented themselves, "his people would be impoverished by their 'paucity of ambition'". And, in parts of Wales, that's just how it has turned out to be.

So what has age got to do with this?

People living now in "generation elderhood" haven't worked in conditions as hostile as coal mines or experienced the poverty of Wales' previous days. But ageism has corroded expectations as effectively as poverty did in the valleys.

This is why we need to be "shell crackers", and "bangers", and "screamers", using whatever opportunities we have. In a very real sense we will be shaping our own destiny because, unless the Lord takes us earlier, we will all be old one day. We are being shaped for elderhood, for those crowns of splendour the Scriptures describe. Elders can behave in such a way and do things that, in strengthening others, help to restore communities. If you are aged over 70 and are reading this you may feel like just an insignificant drop in life's ocean, but the ocean consists only of millions of little drops, and if the little drops that form most of it (the majority population of older people) behaved differently, they could turn the tide.

Chapter 5
How the Tide is Turning

We are living in a post-truth world, we're now told. Hearing it as the topic for a radio discussion, I thought I'd better look up what it meant, because as far as I could see we've been living in a post-truth world for thousands of years already. Isaiah remarked that "our courts oppose the righteous, and justice is nowhere to be found. Truth stumbles in the streets, and honesty has been outlawed" (Isaiah 59:14).

Pontius Pilate, the Roman prefect and politician, was touching on more than he realized when he asked Jesus, "What is truth?" (John 18:38). He didn't wait for an answer. Commentaries vary on why he asked the question, but the Cambridge Bible for Schools and Colleges seems to strike the right note when it describes it as "the half-pitying, half-impatient, question of a practical man of the world, whose experience of life has convinced him that truth is a dream of enthusiasts, and that a kingdom in which truth is to be supreme is as visionary as that of the Stoics". Ellicott's Commentary of 1878 says that other scholars have "seen in it the bitterness of a mind that had been tossed to and fro in the troubled sea of contemporaneous thought, and despaired of an anchorage". Yet standing in front of him was the Revealer of reality, Jesus, the way, the truth, and the life (John 14:6).

The Oxford English Dictionary defines "post-truth" as "an adjective defined as 'relating to or denoting circumstances in which objective facts are less influential in shaping public opinion than appeals to emotion and personal belief'". Looking at the political aspect, Wikipedia says it is "a political culture in which debate is framed largely by appeals to emotion disconnected from the details of policy, and by the repeated assertion of talking points to which factual rebuttals are ignored." Governor Pilate would feel quite at home in this decade, I thought. It explains a lot about ageism, too.

So we are operating on beliefs that are based on feelings that ignore the facts, and each individual's "real world" is a projection of their feelings, not reality. But, in a very real sense, this is nothing new. We mostly base judgments on how we feel, rather than on the facts. One of the reasons cognitive behavioural therapy is so effective is that it teaches individuals how to tell the difference between their emotions and the reality – the facts of the issue. Very early on in the counselling process, clients are introduced to the Thought Challenging Record, a simple form with columns where they note the situation, their feelings, their thoughts, the evidence that supports them, the evidence against them, and a final column for recording how they feel at the end of that exercise. They are learning to separate facts from feelings. When a client begins to make progress and then slips back, more often than not it's because they're not doing their Thought Challenging. After a while you know the Challenge so well you don't need the piece of paper – you can do it in your head. You can find a copy of it here: https://www.getselfhelp. co.uk//docs/ThoughtRecordSheet.pdf Sometimes I think that those behind the intergenerational war described earlier would benefit from a few CBT sessions.

God's life design is a basic fact of life; it is the reality. It's interesting that, as with Pilate, the truth is right under our noses yet we fail to see it. Commenting on the perfect balance and design he sees in medicine, Dr Max Pemberton observes that "it's tempting when studying it to believe in a divine creator because of the way things fit together: the amazingly intricate interplay between chemicals in the body; the unfathomably complex pathways and cascades that underpin physiological function; the translation of genes into proteins; the delicate formation of a foetus from a ball of cells. Everything is in balance, in equilibrium".[36] Richard Dawkins said much the same in *The Blind Watchmaker* (W. W. Norton & Company, 1986), when he warned us not to be deceived by the way things appear to have been designed.

The facts speak for themselves. In this chapter are stories of seniors who are living proof of God's life design, showing as they do how God's purpose for their lives extends to the very end. They also reflect the qualities developed through their lives, and are living with both joy and contentment.

A rustling in the treetops

Who hasn't heard of the fashion magazine *Vogue*? The "bible" of the world of haute couture says that it "places fashion in the context of culture and the world we live in – how we dress, live, and socialize; what we eat, listen to and watch; who leads and inspires us". In other words, it has its finger on its readers' collective pulse, which made its 100th issue all the more extraordinary.

For this once-in-a-lifetime issue, *Vogue* published an

advertisement featuring a 100-year-old woman who had never modelled before. Marjorie "Bo" Gilbert was living in sheltered housing in Birmingham and was discovered on Google by design agency Adam & Eve DBD after an article celebrating her 100th birthday appeared in her local paper. Ben Tollett, the creative director of Adam & Eve DBD, produced the advertisement for fashion house Harvey Nichols. The aim was to highlight and challenge ageism in the fashion industry. He said, "We're really proud to be involved in a project which proves the older generation can be fearlessly stylish too," adding for good measure, "Ageism is so last-century."

Not only was it the first time *Vogue* had featured a 100-year-old, but the advertisement itself was stunning. It was picked up by the media outside the fashion world, who ran it online as well as in their regular print issues. Comments posted beneath the piece on one of the online sites included one from "Carolyn", who said that it was good that *Vogue* recognized that "beauty shines from the inside". "You silly woman," rejoined "Jim". "Did you even *look* at this model? By *any standards* she's a beautiful woman."[37]

Creative directors of world-class advertising agencies are finely tuned to trends and memes, not just today's but those that are creeping over the horizon. They are leaders, not followers, so the advertisement and Ben Tollett's comment were a kind of "rustling in the treetops" (2 Samuel 5:24), a sign that change is coming. Over the past few years we have been seeing more use of models in their 60s and 70s in advertising to match the growing market of older, more discerning consumers, but Bo was the first 100-year-old. She probably won't be the last.

Even Hollywood is taking note of the pulling power of stories featuring older people. Films such as 2015's *The Second Best Exotic Marigold Hotel*, about people retiring to a luxury hotel in India, have been hugely successful. The previous film, *The Best Exotic Marigold Hotel* (2011), was an archetypal coming-of-age comedy, according to the *Telegraph* critic, who said, "The twist [is] the age in question, which was 75-ish." It was a word-of-mouth sales phenomenon, and grossed millions of pounds. There have been other films starring older people since then, and coming shortly, we're told, is a film about a couple on the run from a care home, starring Helen Mirren, 71, and Donald Sutherland, 81.

A surprising author of a stage play about older people was award-winning comedian and broadcaster Sandi Toksvig, who wrote *Silver Lining*, starring a troupe of elderly ladies and a life-and-death rescue mission. She said she had been moved to write *Silver Lining* after becoming concerned about the "lack of respect" shown to the elderly in Britain. It told the story of five elderly women and one young carer, stuck in a Gravesend home amidst rising floods and realizing that "nobody's going to come and save them, because they're dispensable". They decide to mount their own rescue mission, revealing "incredible reserves of knowledge", which leave them "perfectly capable of saving themselves". Sandi Toksvig said she had been inspired by listening to stories from mature actresses, who were struggling to get work and rendered "invisible" to the outside world.[38]

Films and plays like these, including *Quartet*, a 2012 film about retired musicians and singers living in a care home, are attracting more and more mature audiences. It prompted the editor of the *Daily Telegraph* (June 2016) to write that if cinemas really do want to draw older, wiser audiences, then they have to update the whole experience. "No more popcorn and soda, but a nice glass of wine," he suggested. "We demand change! It's called the silver screen for a reason." On the other hand, an inspection of the audience for the new genre of computer-generated children's films with their sophisticated humour and clever stories shows a good number of seniors with their grandchildren, so perhaps the popcorn should stay.

* * * *

Teach young people that we are not going to move over

This was the bold newspaper headline topping a photograph of four smiling ladies in their 70s, sitting on a bench in a sunlit town square. They may have been smiling but they wanted it to be known that they were no longer going to step off a sidewalk to let teenagers hurtle by on cycles or rollerblades or step aside for youngsters with their heads down over their phones, as they'd been forced to do so often in the past. These are Baby Boomers, who have brought their non-conformist, oppositional mindsets into their "third" age and are not going to put up with disrespect or invisibility.

The article by the *Guardian* was part of a series looking at ageing populations in cities.[39] Older people all over the world were asked for their views. Wherever they lived, in whatever city, how did they think it could be improved for older citizens? The responses were very telling. Many responded with similar, practical ideas, such as wide and level pavements, efficient and affordable bus services, lower kerbs, public toilets, handrails, good lighting and signage – things that help seniors to move safely from one place to another, to keep up with friends, and to stay part of the community.

One interviewee said, "An age-friendly city makes it easy to move about by transit, or walking, without being hurried for fear of being run over by a car, or pushed over by a young person using a mobile. Reduce the number of cars. Slow them down. Give walking the first priority. Teach young people that we are not going to move over, nor do we have to."

Keep cyclists off the sidewalks, said several. The correspondent from Canada emphasized the need for security and respect for older people who walk, a sentiment echoed by another from America. The person from Seattle said that it was important to ensure that drivers and cyclists respect a walker's right of way: so keep cyclists off the sidewalks. "Traffic-related anxiety discourages older people from leaving their homes, and getting the many benefits that come from walking. This fosters both poor health and social isolation. What are needed are tolerance, patience, and acceptance of people as they are."

The comment from a New Yorker raises a big smile. I used to visit New York when I worked for a global publisher, and can tell you that its sidewalks are the hardest in the world. They are made of concrete poured onto solid rock and have no spring in them whatsoever. Rivers of people in trainers stride along them each day from the subway to the office. But never mind the sidewalks; the New York correspondent said, "I'd like to see reduced prices for seniors at restaurants, movies, museums, etc., as well as more public benches and buses that lower their entries for those who can't manage higher steps." Reduced prices for the essentials – so New York!

And, significantly, people did not want to be segregated by age. "I believe it's important for all ages to interact on a day-to-day basis," said one. "It gives everyone a much richer and broader experience and hopefully removes the labelling of people as 'elderly' or 'past it' and the self-fulfilling behaviours that are often generated by this." "Self-fulfilling behaviours" is a very perceptive observation. This came from Australia, a very youth-oriented country, so the suggestion was that any physical aids should be included discreetly in city infrastructure. Then they would help not just older people but those with disabilities, too, and people with babies and small children. This infrastructure would include entrances that are easy to get in and out of, additional seating here and there, reliable transport that people want to use, public toilets that are clean and safe, and removing trip hazards on paths and roads, or, if that is not possible, highlighting them. "Then people of all ages can have as safe, active, and socially connected a lifestyle as possible."

Avoiding loneliness and staying socially connected was seen to be vital. "My neighbourhood is purely residential: no convenient supermarkets and very poor public transport facilities," said a 70-year-old from Manchester, England. "So transport is essential. Without my own car I would be almost totally cut off. Here in Manchester there is an abundance of things to be involved with for all ages – but all this is dependent on the costs involved and the ability to get to the venue. So the city is inclusive if you have the money to pay for the facilities, and would be accessible if the transport arrangements were improved." Good transport networks, especially buses, are becoming more and more of a problem in Britain as services are cut because of austerity measures. People in rural areas are the worst hit. It is a false economy, as feelings of loneliness increase the risk of dementia by 47 per cent among older people, so it is simply an expedient shifting of costs from one silo today to another tomorrow. Cut spending on public transport today and pay more in dementia care costs tomorrow.

* * * *

Energized to dream great things

At the age of 70 and pondering retirement, author and preacher John Piper wrote that he was "energized to dream great things, because this year Hillary turns 69, Bernie turns 75, and Donald turns 70". His increasing energy was due to the "incredible fact that all of them want to spend their seventies doing the hardest job in the world". He saw this as "wonderfully countercultural". But his mission was bigger than theirs. They were only after being president of the country of the USA, but he sees himself as being an ambassador of the Sovereign of the universe. "They only get to change the way some people live for a few decades. I get to change the way some people live for ever – with a lot of good spill-over for this world in the process."[40]

He listed people who have achieved great things in their later years. Winston Churchill wrote *A History of the English-Speaking Peoples* at the age of 82. Ronald Reagan served as president from age 70 to 78. Three of America's Supreme Court judges are over the age of 75. Grandma Moses started painting at the age of 77: Goethe finished writing his famous *Faust* when he was 82, and at the age of 89 Albert Schweitzer was running a hospital in Africa.

Piper writes, "'The righteous… still bear fruit in old age… to declare that the Lord is upright' (Psalm 92:12–15, NKJV). Why would God tell us that? Because he wants us to dream that. He wants us to pray for that." He acknowledges that not everyone gets this privilege. Some die young. Some must bear the burden of immobilizing pain. "It's sad to think that with today's advanced medicine people suffer immobilizing pain, and I hope they are few." But, as you'll read, immobilization by itself does not prevent you from living fully in God's plan. In my last book[41] I mentioned Michael Denman, a retired vicar who is largely confined to a wheelchair but who is as alive in Christ as any man I've met. And later on you'll read about George, a former college basketball star who, at the height of his career, was brought low by a slow, paralysing disease. Years into the disease, dependent on carers 24 hours a day and completely immobile, "breathing" through a tracheostomy and communicating by touching a special keypad with his knee, George told his neurosurgeon that he was happy to be alive; he was grateful and his life was full. He was in touch with others via the computer – networking, advising, and encouraging.

About a year ago, knowing I would be writing this book, I started collecting stories of older people contributing to life, and now have bulging files full of them. But there are too many in all, so I'm only able to mention a few. They're becoming the rule, rather than the exception. They are like little lights that are so numerous they're shining a pathway to "where it's at", as some of my American friends would say. They pop up everywhere –

in the media and on Facebook, Twitter, and YouTube. Many are known to me personally from my work.

These little lights are not put out by frailty and poor health. Every year, the Pilgrims' Friend Society holds a dedicated, countrywide day of prayer. Everyone is involved – trustees, directors, line managers and home managers, supporters, volunteers, and residents – everybody. One year, 104-year-old Violet, living in our care home in Harrogate, contributed the lead prayer for the day's programme. Violet had been a believer since the age of 21, and said she had sent up many a prayer over the years, especially for her family. She said, "My prayer for this nation is that they would include God in their lives more. I think it has become a godless country with church only on special occasions and not taken seriously. It makes all the difference when you start leaving the Lord out. I pray that they would know the Foursquare Gospel – Saviour, Baptizer with the Holy Spirit, Healer, Soon-coming King. I pray that they would trust and believe in the Lord like I do because He never lets you down, He's always faithful. Bless the Lord".

Only this morning I received an email from a pastoral worker in Nottingham who mentioned, almost in passing, that last Sunday a 94-year-old had given an inspiring word when he'd preached the sermon at church. Tell me more, I requested. She replied that Douglas is a retired pastor who still writes notes for The Geneva Bible Studies: "Although his sight is failing he has a wealth of biblical and pastoral ministry and knowledge, which he shares with such a warm heart of understanding. He is a treasure. He is married to Hilda and they are both living independently at home with some help."

In my own church, apart from the pastor (who is truly anointed), one of the clearest, most interesting speakers is 85-year-old Paul, who from his experiences and deep knowledge of scripture draws out treasures both new and old. Paul has been a church builder and pastor all his life, and although he doesn't have the best of health has a ministry of fathering and supporting today's pastors. He and his wife, Ruth, are sought for their spiritual wisdom by people of all ages. They are set to lead a Marriage Enrichment course shortly.

Still singing praises to God at the age of 96 is Royal Air Force veteran Dennis Doyle. He has been singing in his local choir since he joined it in 1927, initially as a treble.[42] It's the 43,000 hymns and more than 4,300 choir practices over the years that have kept him feeling young, he says. "It keeps me going, and I have quite an active lifestyle where I am out, involved in music, almost every day of the week. I really enjoy it. I still write music now but it takes me a bit longer than it used to – I have to think of something for inspiration." Dennis attended Fitzwilliam College, Cambridge as an associate in music, and also studied music at Trinity College London. The Director of Studies in Music at Fitzwilliam, Francis Knights, said that their singers and music students have really benefited from his encouragement and gifts.

What is old?

Pop over to YouTube, and have a look at these pacesetters. You can see Eileen Ash, a former cricketer, now 105 years old and doing yoga moves that would do credit to someone half her age. "It improves your brain and your muscles," she said. Asked if she woke up with aches and pains she said, "No, not yet. Perhaps when I get old. But – what is old?" Here she is, at https://www.youtube.com/watch?v=dKji0oK1bmg

While you're on the YouTube site you might like to look up Britain's oldest poppy seller, 99-year-old Ron Jones. Ron was a prisoner of war in Auschwitz, and was one of the hundreds forced to join the "death march" of prisoners across Europe in 1945. Most of his comrades in the Welch Regiment died, and for 40 years he's been selling poppies "so that people will remember what has gone before them". The supermarket where he works is not far from me, and I met him there four years ago, when he was only 96. He told me about the march, and how his wife had cried on his return when she saw the living skeleton he had become. She nursed him back to health, he said. https://www.youtube.com/watch?v=4hj0Rie80gk

Polish runner Stanislaw Kowalsky, 104, set a new European record for the 100 metres, running it in 9.58 seconds. You can see him limbering up and running on YouTube at http://www.dailymail.co.uk/video/football/video-1094806/104-year-old-Stanislaw-Kowalski-completes-100-metre-sprint.html

Making the television news was sprinter Tony Bowman, 80, who ran the 100 metres just five seconds more slowly than Usain Bolt, the fastest man in the world.[43] Tony won six out of the eight UK sprinting records for his age group after he'd overcome heart disease (having had stents inserted). One of his ambitions is to run the 100 metres when he is 100 years old, and then to live for another 20 years. Later in 2016, the same year he won the 100 metres, he set a benchmark of 10.86 seconds for the 60 metres hurdles when he competed at the British Indoor

Championships in London. He said, "I was absolutely over the moon. It is my first world record ever – it took me 80 years to get it," adding, "It has given me a great lift. But I still want to continue as long as possible, God willing."[44]

Then there is 106-year-old Sam Martinez, one of Scotland's oldest men, who said the secret to his long life was his love of cooking. He left his native Belize in 1942 to go to Scotland to work as a forester, helping in the war effort, and decided to stay. When interviewed in May 2016, he was mostly looking after himself, cooking favourite dishes such as cock-a-leekie soup, fish and chips, and haggis, but he also made big pots of soup for his family. He was an ardent supporter of his local football team, Hibernian, and when he died in August 2016 the team wore black armbands at their next game as a mark of their affection for him.[45]

Australian environmental scientist Dr David Goodall, 102, has produced more than 100 research papers in an ecology research and teaching career spanning 70 years, and at the time of writing (2016) is still working at Western Australia's Edith Cowan University. Interviewed by BBC Radio, his responses were quick and lively. He intends to continue working because he wants to continue to contribute to the body of scientific knowledge on his subject.

Anthony Horowitz and his wife, a television producer, flew for a long weekend to Palm Springs to meet the author Herman Wouk, the Pulitzer-Prize-winning author of *The Winds of War*, *The Caine Mutiny*, and others, in the hope that they could persuade him to let them make a television series based on *The Caine Mutiny*. When they met Mr Wouk they found him behind his desk, working on his latest novel. He interrogated them in detail for two hours, an "inquisition that showed how carefully he had checked us out before we arrived". "But this is the remarkable thing," wrote Horowitz. "In a few days' time he was going to be 99 years old!"

Ninety-six-year-old Jewish peer saving Christians

Who could have failed to be moved by 96-year-old Lord Weidenfeld, the publisher and philanthropist, writing about his mission to save Christians threatened by terrorists in the Middle East? "Powerful, eloquent and utterly gripping... Jewish peer, 96, on his mission to stop IS massacre of innocents," the editor had entitled it.[46] Lord Weidenfeld was sent by his family to safety in Britain in 1938 when Austria was no longer a safe place to be a Jew. He arrived at Dover with one suitcase and 16 shillings and sixpence, and was "billeted in a desperate boarding house in King's Cross, surviving on a handout of £2 a week. Yet here I am, now 96, chairman of Weidenfeld & Nicolson, the publishing house I founded, a peer of the realm, a man who has been counsellor to heads of state, a Jew privileged to count himself as a friend of a crusading pope".

He says he owes it all to a family of evangelical Christians who took him in. "They gave me a bed and put meals on the table." They supported him in his studies and his work, and vouched for his parents to the Home Office so that they, too, could find sanctuary in London. The three were able to begin their lives anew, and Lord Weidenfeld felt it was a debt he would never be able to repay. In 2015 he launched the Weidenfeld Fund to help rescue 2,000 families from the IS terror – around 10,000 souls. The fund operates by supporting the work of Christian charity the Barnabas Fund. "Put simply, we rely on a Christian network to deal with the logistics, while we, a Jewish network, raise money to help pay the bills," he said. Quoting Pope Paul II, who used to say that "the Jew is the elder brother of the Church", Lord Weidenfeld averred that "this Christmas it is time for us to look after our younger siblings".

* * * *

Gleams of the dawn

"The way of the righteous is like the first gleam of dawn, which shines ever brighter until the full light of day," says Proverbs 4:18. There are so many "gleams of dawn" shining light along the seniors' pathway that they could fill a book on their own.

David Chapman, 95, and his wife, also 95, were missionary workers and business people all their adult lives. In 2011, David published an autobiographical book called *The Little Things*, a title taken from the last words of David, the patron saint of Wales: "Brothers and sisters, be full of joy! Keep your faith and guard your belief! Do those little things, which you have learned from me and seen in me."

For the past few years David and his wife have been living in a care home in South Wales. The home is beautifully managed by Christians, yet David was keen to see more support for the home from believers in local churches. He knew how much PFS support groups do for our residents, and his aim was to create a similar ministry. So he emailed leaders of local churches, outlining his ideas and inviting them to a launch of the "Friends" meeting. He ran the whole thing, even putting a press story about the event in the local newspaper, which published it in its entirety, without a sign of sub-editing.

When we were looking for people to trial our programme of cognitive and spiritual stimulation for older people, "Brain and Soul Boosting for Seniors", David obtained a copy, enlisted the help of a retired GP in her 80s who is one of our supporters, and arranged for the sessions to be run with residents at the home. After the first few sessions he emailed to say that it was a great success. David's wife has dementia, and his own health is not without challenges, but he is still one of those "gleams of dawn".

* * * *

If only one dog could yodel

These are just a few examples of older people living life to the full, and the only exceptional thing about them, except perhaps the competition winners, is that their stories have been published. But Dr Ellen Langer, Professor of Psychology at Harvard University, would argue that even if they were exceptions – even if there were only a handful of older people like this – that fact alone would still declare the truth that lives like theirs are possible for us all.

"If only one dog could yodel," she wrote in her book *Counterclockwise*, that would show that yodelling is possible in dogs."[47] Dr Langer has a particular interest in the psychology of ageing, in particular how our thoughts influence our bodies. In Chapter 6 we look at how an experiment she and her team conducted with a group of older men showed how changing their thinking rowed back their physical conditions by up to 20 years – their eyesight, blood pressure, walking, and cognition all *measurably* improved. Dr Langer's work asks how our belief in our physical limits constrains us. Do we simply accept the received wisdom, or do we look for the possibilities outside it?

In Mark 5, we find the synagogue leader Jairus, who chose to believe Jesus in the face of all evidence to the contrary (John 8:50). It was only after he'd returned home that he found his faith confirmed and that his daughter was, in fact, alive and well. The "gleams of dawn" people mentioned here are illustrations of God's plan for old age. He means it to be a glorious chapter in our lives, when we have time to know Him' more closely, radiate His faithfulness, and, by accepting the role of elderhood designed for His seniors, bless the world.

Chapter 6
How Not to Be Knackered at 90

Let me explain this word "knackered." It's an English colloquial expression described by the Urban Dictionary as a "word used to describe a person or object that is spent beyond all reasonable use as in 'He is only fit for the knacker's yard'". The knacker's yard was where injured and worn-out horses were taken to be slaughtered. "Spent beyond all reasonable use" and "worn out to the point of extinction" are encapsulated in this one word, and I haven't found another that does the job as well.

I wanted to call this book *How Not to Be Knackered at 90*, but discovered that there's another unsavoury connotation to the word, although it's not widely known. I tested it with people of all ages and discovered that most thought, as I did, that it meant "worn out, too weak to go to work". The only person who expressed a real distaste for the word was a dear friend and one of the sharpest media lawyers in London, who said it made him think of the horrors of what happened to these knacker's-yard horses. When I ran it by my pastor, he said he knew people who were knackered at 40, never mind 90. "To the pure in heart, all is pure," I thought, but so as not to give offence in anything (2 Corinthians 6:3), it was abandoned as a title. But now I've explained it I'll use the word as shorthand to describe the condition no one wants to experience at any age, especially when you're 90. It is something you definitely do not want to be, and in this chapter we look at how to avoid it.

In the previous chapter were stories of people who were 90 and older, but who weren't knackered. They may have had arthritis, creaky knees, and some of the various ailments that come with old age, but they were not "spent beyond all reasonable use". So what was it about them; what did they have that brought them to that place – and how can we prepare now, whatever age we are, for those "best of life" senior years? It should begin no later than one's teens, said Dwight Moody, the great 19th-century evangelist. So the time to start is *now*.

What really matters isn't so much the state of the body, but the health of the soul and the spirit. The apostle Paul refers to the body, soul, and spirit in his letter to the Christians at Thessalonica, when he writes, "Now may the God of peace Himself sanctify you entirely; and may your spirit and soul and body be preserved complete, without blame at the coming of our Lord Jesus Christ" (1 Thessalonians 5:23, NASB). For a believer, the health of the spirit determines the health of the soul – and the health of the soul can, in turn, have an impact on the health of the physical body. We are, essentially, spirit beings in "earthly tents" (2 Corinthians 5:1), marvellously made altogether. A beautiful illustration is Ramandu, the ancient man whom the children meet in C. S. Lewis's *The Voyage of the Dawn Treader*, who says he is a retired star. Eustace challenges Ramandu, saying, "In our world a star is a huge ball of flaming gas". In reply, Ramandu answers, "Even in your world, my son, that is not what a star is but only what it is made of."

* * * *

They say you know you're growing old when you look in the mirror and see your mother's face looking back at you. But in my case I'm not so blessed. My mother was quite beautiful, whereas I look more like my eccentric Aunt Amelia. She and her eccentricities were as much a given in our family as the post box on the corner, so much so that when I was a child I thought every family had a "batty" aunt. But, more to the point, Aunt Amelia had the family face with features that all of us share in some way. One of our characteristics is that we don't get wrinkles as we grow older – none of us have that sort of skin. But we do have a sort of landslide; a kind of gentle heading south that causes things to droop – eyes, noses, knees, chins, and jowls, those sorts of things. We ignore it, of course, although occasionally one of us might mention casually in conversation people who have the courage and the money for cosmetic surgery. The truth is that none of us really knows what we look like, partly because it's a subjective evaluation and partly because we don't see our faces when they're animated in the company of others. However, how our older relatives turn out can sometimes give us a hint of how we might age, physically and psychologically.

Our families are the chrysalis from which we emerge with a firm view of other people, the world, and, most importantly, ourselves. The quality of our parenting, and in particular our emotional connections in those early years, embeds within our souls a set of beliefs about others, the world in general, and ourselves. Mapping out these three points is like drawing a triangular tectonic plate on which our personality rests. In cognitive behavioural therapy, these beliefs are called "schemas" – deeply ingrained core beliefs, which can be healthy or dysfunctional. Dysfunctional schemas produce negative thoughts, and these in turn produce negative emotions. I never fail to be amazed by how strong and lasting these schemas can be, even in people in their 60s or 70s or beyond. It's as the Scripture says: "'Train up a child in the way he should go, and when he is old he will not depart from it" (Proverbs 22:6, NKJV).

At three years of age a child's tectonic plate is so developed that neuroscientists can predict with reasonable accuracy those who will go on to have unsatisfactory lives, being a burden on the state's resources because of criminality, antisocial behaviour, being unemployed, and having long-term poor health.[48] They comprise just 20 per cent of the population but will consume 80 per cent of the state's resources, owing to crime, health problems, and unemployment. In a 45-minute test, neuroscientists at Duke University, New Zealand found the strongest factors were deprivation and "brain health", measured by intelligence, motor skills, language abilities, restlessness, susceptibility to being frustrated, and lack of perseverance – that latter measure alone being a major predictor of the success, or otherwise, of their future lives. As you've persevered with this rather thought-provoking book so far, you're unlikely to be one of the unfortunate 20 per cent.

The power of perseverance and purpose

Perseverance is one of the most important attributes of successful living in old age, or, indeed, at any time of life. In business, pundits say it's the key to success. In his letter to the Christians at Rome Paul reminded them that persevering through difficult times builds character, and that proven character produces hope, "and hope does not disappoint, because the love of God has been poured out within our hearts through the Holy Spirit who was given to us" (Romans 5:3–5, NASB). So the ability to persevere is both a sign of character and at the same time something that builds character. It's important to know this because our character as seniors will sustain us and help us become the elders that God intends us to be. So how is it that some people will persevere, and some will give up?

Two of my friends are evangelists, and are currently running a programme of social engagement, building communities in deprived areas. It doesn't operate under a Christian flag so as to avoid being seen as proselytizing (which it isn't; it's about restoring communities), but, as my friend says, "Salt is salt whatever you call it." The husband was a successful businessman before the Lord called him and his wife into full-time ministry. At the time they had four young children and a mortgage, but they believed that as God had called them to the work, He would provide all they needed. One of their treasured keepsakes is a tape recording of a prophetic word that was sung to them by the musician leading worship at a Christian retreat we attended, where each line confirmed their calling and even the name of the work. Towards the end, almost as an afterthought, the musician sang, "And yes, you will be paid."

In the following years they paid their mortgage, put the children through university, and, they would say, lived well. But it hasn't been plain sailing. In recent years they've known more tough times than ever; times that seemed to last longer than when they first started out. They've come close to giving up, especially when a good business offer came along. What kept them going was the sense of purpose that God had given them, and their expectations, based on their past experiences with Him, that He had called them and that He would sustain them. They also have a deep relationship with Jesus and they knew, really knew, that He loved them.

Today, they make leaps of faith that take my breath away, but, for them, each time it's easier because they've become stronger through each experience. It's as it says in Jeremiah: "If you have run with footmen and they have tired you out, then how can you compete with horses? If you fall down in a land of peace, how will you do in the thicket of the Jordan?" (Jeremiah 12:5, NASB). It's going to get tougher, not easier, God is telling Jeremiah.

We are the beneficiaries of the most extreme example in the universe of persevering in the face of overwhelming circumstances. Matthew describes Jesus' agony in the Garden, of enduring the horror of knowing all that was to come, but still persevering with His Father's purpose for Him. The writer of Hebrews urges, "Let us run with endurance the race God has set before us. Because of the joy awaiting him, he endured the cross, disregarding its shame. Now he is seated in the place of honour beside God's throne." What glory! Jesus fulfilled His purpose.

Apart from taking the Creator out of the picture, one of the saddest things about Darwin's Theory of Evolution is that if we believe that we are all here by chance, it blinds us to the fact that we are here by divine design. If you know that you are here for a purpose, even if you don't know what your specific role or work is at this moment, you will be content to let it come to you.

A key verse for understanding this is Ephesians 2:10: "For we are His workmanship, created in Christ Jesus for good works, which God prepared beforehand that we would walk in them" (NKJV). We are created and equipped for "good works". Some works will be big and some will be small, and I believe that if we could see the ripple effects of the little things, the compound interest they accumulate, we would be amazed. One of our popular seminars is "Developing your gifts and equipping in old age", or "Developing usefulness in old age", and we often find people floundering as they seek useful things to do. We say – don't worry about that! God has made you a round peg and the round holes will come along as you continue on your pilgrimage.

Knowing that we are here for a purpose gives us resilience, the ability to plough through and bounce back from adversity. We know that we're not on our own, left to our own devices. It gives us a sense of coherence; a knowing that, whatever happens in life, its demands are worthy of investment and engagement.

Firing on all cylinders

To enjoy our senior years to the full and to take up our roles as elders we need to examine our hearts, as the Psalmist said, and make sure that they are not harbouring anxious thoughts, or a "hurtful way" (Psalm 139, NASB). "Hurtful ways" include anxiety, which is another name for fear. It is probably the biggest single reason that people seek counselling. Unremitting anxiety leads to depression; in peeling back the layers in counselling, people often find that beneath depression lies anxiety. And beneath anxiety is often a lack of confidence in oneself, and one's ability to cope. Cognitive behavioural therapy uses Socratic questioning to help the person discover the root of the problem, and when I discussed this one day with my college tutor he said that, in his many years of counselling and learning, he had found that underlying the majority of emotional problems is a lack of self-worth. Christians can be conflicted about this, because some are taught that we're not worth anything because we are sinners. But we are so valuable to God that He gave everything He had to bring us back to Himself. Jesus said that He has even numbered the hairs on our heads.

It raises the question – how is it that some people have self-confidence, and others don't? Often it's down to our development in our early years. Our personalities are set for life by the time we are six years old, and we stay recognizably the same person, across time and contexts.

Jane was in her early 60s when she came for counselling. On the surface she seemed to be fine: she was intelligent, with a good job and a long, happy marriage, but she lived every day with levels of anxiety that drained her energy. She couldn't leave home without being immaculate in every way and everything she did at work had to be perfect. She'd had counselling before so knew the root cause was that her mother had been a perfectionist, desperately trying to keep up with the Joneses in an area she felt was "above her". Her house, her garden, and her children always had to be perfect. Ingrained in Jane's tectonic plate, her schema, was the belief that she would not be acceptable unless she was seen to be perfect. The slightest flaw, even not wearing make-up, was to be less than perfect.

Underneath the perfection Jane felt incredibly vulnerable, and her negative thoughts restricted her life severely. She was like a hummingbird, expending so much energy on just staying in position that she would arrive home from work and go to bed within an hour. By the weekend, she said, she was "knackered".

She believed that her colleagues held low opinions of her, so we agreed she would do a behaviour experiment. We drew up a little questionnaire that she would ask her colleagues to complete as part of a self-discovery project. When she saw the results, she was astounded to find that, as well as being seen as reliable and having integrity, she was strongly liked and admired, and even seen as a role model by some. Going back to the aeroplane engine analogy, we could say that one cylinder she hadn't been firing on was now clear and she had more thrust to go forward, because that's exactly what happened.

Negative thoughts are like the birds that fly into planes' engines and disempower them, but we don't have to live with them. Several Scriptures help: Galatians 5:16 tells us to "let the Holy Spirit guide your lives. Then you won't be doing what your sinful nature craves" (NLT). "Walking in the Spirit" helps identify and combat the negative thoughts that produce the "hurtful ways", the anxiety, guilt, anger, depression, and so on. The Scriptures have power, and are not simply words on paper: "For the word of God is alive and powerful. It is sharper than the sharpest two-edged sword, cutting between soul and spirit, between joint and marrow. It exposes our innermost thoughts and desires" (Hebrews 4:12).

It helps to write appropriate Scripture verses on Post-it™ notes that you can put in places where you'll see them at different times of the day – on the bathroom mirror, tucked inside your laptop bag, inside a kitchen cupboard, and so on. The book of Philippians is very helpful: "I can do all things through Him who strengthens me" (Philippians 4:13, NASB). Some other useful verses are 1 Peter 5:7: "[Cast] all your anxiety on Him, because He cares for you"; 2 Samuel 22:30: "For by You I can run against a troop; by my God I can leap over a wall"; and Psalm 138:8 (ESV): "The Lord will fulfil his purpose for me; your steadfast love, O Lord, endures forever. Do not forsake the work of your hands", which is confirmed by Ephesians 2:10; and there are many more. In the 1994 film *Forrest Gump*, the hero's mother tells him that life is like a box of chocolates and you don't know what they're like until you unwrap them. Do you remember the old sherbet sweets that after a moment or two in your mouth released a burst of flavour so big it would take you by surprise? Scripture verses are like that: as you dwell on them they release bursts of well-being into your spirit. But, unlike the sherbet sweets, which lasted just for a moment, the Holy Spirit soaks into your innermost being and releases comfort and strength.

Renewing the spirit of the mind

Jill Bolte Taylor is an extraordinarily dedicated neuroscientist. One of her hobbies is making works of art by etching intricate neuronal circuitry on glass, and some hang in the lobby of Harvard University, where she works. The importance of guarding our hearts and weeding out "hurtful ways" is described by her in *My Stroke of Insight*, the book she wrote about her journey of recovery after suffering a massive brain haemorrhage. At one point she discovered that, as parts of the left hemisphere of her brain came back to life, "old files" were opened, and some of her negative emotional baggage surfaced. She'd been blissfully happy without the argumentative, critical, must-always-be-right thinking and, as only a neuroscientist could put it, she wrote that she needed to "evaluate the usefulness of preserving its underlying neural circuit". In other words, unhelpful baggage was not to have a place in her brain; it was not wanted on the rest of her journey.

Understanding how her neural circuitry worked, she declared, "No one had the power to make me feel anything except for me and my brain." And she asserted that, although she was not going to be in total control of what happened to her in her life, "I am certainly in charge of how I choose to perceive my experience". "I made the cognitive choice to stay out of my own way during the process of recovery," she wrote, "being very careful about my self-talk."[49]

A similar practical approach is taken by cognitive neuroscientist Dr Caroline Leaf in her book *Who Switched Off My Brain?*[50] The book outlines the pathology of our thinking processes and how our choices influence our neuronal health, or otherwise. Eric Kandel is a neuropsychiatrist who won a Nobel Prize for his work on signal transduction in the nervous system.[51] Listening to him talking to Charlie Rose (one of the world's best interviewers) on Bloomberg TV one evening, I was struck by Kandel's assertion that "when you go to bed at night, your thoughts that day have constructed your brain". I've never heard anyone as eminent as Kandel say as clearly as that that your thoughts shape your brain. It echoes Tom Kitwood, the trailblazer in dementia care, who claimed that everything that happens in our lives – every transaction, every perception – is a neuronal event.[52] It also chimes with the growing understanding of the "plasticity" of the brain.

It also highlights the wisdom of Philippians 4:8, which tells us to dwell on "what is true, noble, righteous, pure, lovable or admirable, on some virtue or on something praiseworthy" (CJB). One of my relatives is always a "glass half empty" person, with a mindset that instinctively leans towards the negative. I say to him, "In life there are negatives, and there are positives. One drags you down, one doesn't. We can choose what to dwell on."

The warning in Job

"What I always feared has happened to me. What I dreaded has come true. I have no peace, no quietness," said Job (Job 3:25–26). There are such things as self-fulfilling prophecies, as Proverbs 4:23 warns: "Guard your heart above all else, for it determines the course of your life."

In a study of personality, ageing, and longevity, American psychologist Becca Levy and her colleagues looked at the lives of a group of more than 650 people who, in 1975, had been asked to respond to positive and negative statements about ageing. They could agree or disagree with thoughts such as "Things keep getting worse as I get older", "As you get older, you are less useful", and "I am as happy now as I was when I was younger".

Checking the records of the participants more than 20 years later, Levy and her colleagues found that those who viewed ageing more positively lived, on average, seven and a half years longer than those who were negative about it. "Simply having a positive attitude made far more difference than any to be gained from lowering blood pressure or reducing cholesterol, which typically improve lifespan by about four years. It also beats the benefits of exercise, maintaining proper weight, and not smoking, which are found to add one to three years."[53]

It was the dread of being old that caused a perfectly healthy 75-year-old former nurse to travel to Switzerland for assisted suicide. Gill Pharaoh, who had specialized in nursing the elderly, was afraid she might have a stroke when she was older and be unable to care for herself. She said she preferred euthanasia to becoming "an old lady hobbling up the road with a trolley".[54] Her life was in decline, she said, as she did not enjoy late dinner parties any more, or gardening, and had tinnitus. She was leaving behind a husband and two daughters, and acknowledged that her decision was not what they wanted. But she did not believe in "gods" and felt that the age of 70 was a normal lifespan. She was aware that there are wonderful men and women who are busy and active and enjoying life well beyond 80 or 90 years of age, but saw them as lucky exceptions. It was a sad story, and no one seemed to have asked her how she could be sure she wouldn't be one of the "fortunate ones". Being physically independent was the most important thing to her, more than the love of her husband and children. Without it, she was knackered – she had no purpose in life, no reason to persevere.

At a Christmas meal for older people, Roger Hitchings met a very intelligent and rational 87-year-old. Roger said, "He had recently recovered from treatment for cancer and was thankful for good health. But then he made this outrageous statement: 'I really think it was wrong of them to keep me alive. I am 87 and of no real value to anybody. And in the light of the limited resources why didn't they just let me die? I don't want to die but now I am living I am a drain on society. I've had my time. The animal kingdom is much wiser than we are; they exclude the old and leave them to fade away.' He was not a believer and it was impossible to deal with all he said, but what became clear was that he was totally influenced by the media presentation and evolutionary thinking."

There are people for whom the opposite is true. People like Joni Eareckson Tada, who became quadriplegic after a diving accident when she was 17. Now 67, Joni is a successful disability rights activist, a recognized painter (she paints with a paintbrush between her teeth), and the author of over 40 books. The first book sold more than four million copies and was translated into 50 languages, and was the beginning of her evangelical ministry, Joni and Friends. In her early 60s, she battled breast cancer. If anyone could be justified in giving up, it would be Joni! But she didn't – her face shows a joyful spirit. She is far from knackered. She tells her story on YouTube, at https://www.youtube.com/watch?v=VVXJ8GyLgt0

Against all the odds

One of the most extreme examples of persevering in spite of overwhelming circumstances was that of George Kalomiris, and his wife, Felicity. When Boston neurosurgeon Allan Ropper first met George, he thought he looked as if he'd stepped out of the pages of *Sports Illustrated*. He was 6' 4" tall, an avid basketball player, with the impressive physique that had made him a college basketball star. He had a successful career and Felicity, a lawyer, had just landed a good job. They had a new baby and a new house. Then George began to experience a series of sudden, inexplicable weaknesses that led to his appointment with Dr Ropper and a diagnosis of Lou Gehrig's disease or amyotrophic lateral sclerosis (ALS, known in the UK as motor neurone disease or MND), a progressive neurodegenerative disease that causes muscle weakness, paralysis, and, ultimately, respiratory failure.

They learned about the likely progression of the disease and the points at which George could decide whether or not to have life-extending interventions, such as the ventilator. They discussed it at length, and questioned whether at some point, unable to move and locked into your body, you are no longer worth anything. Are you no longer a human being? Are you no longer really alive at that point? Felicity said, "I remember telling George that I fell in love with him because of his soul, and that I knew his soul – his essence, his spirit, what defined him as a man – was going to remain intact whatever happened to him physically." George decided he wanted to live every second available to him to experience the love and friendship of his wife and his daughter. Looking back, years later, he said that he had a reason and a purpose to "stick around".

Ten years after the diagnosis, Dr Ropper visited them at home. George was by then 95 per cent paralysed, confined to a specially designed wheelchair with his head strapped back to keep it from falling forward. He was connected to a ventilator, and needed a carer 24 hours a day. He communicated via a computer, operated by the touch of one knee, which he also used to write letters and emails, and converse with his wife and daughter. Teaching his daughter, Sophie, how to communicate with him boosted her language skills to the point where she could read a 500-page book in the second grade.

Despite the paralysis, George kept busy every day. He was involved with fund-raising organizations and research organizations, and networking with others with ALS. He wrote letters and did the household shopping online. Felicity had coped with breast cancer and, a year later, thyroid cancer. She said their chief priorities were "maintaining our moral and spiritual compass, our health and wellbeing and that of our daughter, and maintaining my livelihood". Some of their friends fell away, but those who "were able to look into the ugly face of ALS and not turn away came to realize that the essence of George had survived this calamity, and for that they have been blessed with the ongoing gift of his love, his humour, his friendship, and an inspiration for life that comes from being around him". Dr Ropper remarked on how "normal" the atmosphere was in their home. After ten years of coping with ALS, breast cancer, thyroid cancer, and the myriad adjustments and challenges, George and Felicity Kalomiris were not knackered.[55]

* * * *

As a man thinks in his heart, so he is

Social psychologist Ellen Langer was the first female professor to gain tenure in the Psychology Department at Harvard University. One of her pressing questions was, "Could we change our physical health by changing our minds?" She and her team devised a study which they called "the Counterclockwise Study". They took groups of eight men in their 80s on a week-long retreat in a house that had been retrofitted and taken back to 1959. Every item in the house belonged to that era. All the men were interviewed beforehand and took baseline physical and psychological tests. They were thoroughly briefed and prepared. The "experimental group" were to live in the house as though they were living in 1959. They were not to bring any books, newspapers, or family pictures that were from later than 1959. They were to go back in time, to turn their minds back and live in that year, not discussing anything that had happened after 1959. The team carefully studied what life was like in 1959 – the politics and social issues, the TV shows – everything they would have encountered in that year that would effectively take participants back to it. Participants and researchers met daily, discussed events that were happening, and watched films of the era. (It was a time when an IBM computer filled a whole room, and pantyhose had just been introduced.)

The control group that came separately another week was just to enjoy the week and reminisce about 1959.

What happened? After each week-long retreat the team tested the participants and found that the mind does indeed have enormous control over the body. Both groups, the experimental and the control, came out of the experience with their hearing and their memory, even the strength of their grip, significantly improved. On many of the measures, the participants got younger. In the experimental group fingers lengthened as arthritis diminished and they were able to move them more, and they had greater manual dexterity. There were improvements in height, weight, gait, posture, and scores in intelligence tests. Finally, independent observers who were unaware of the experiment were asked to examine the photographs taken before and after the week's retreat. "Those objective observers judged that all those experimental participants looked noticeably younger at the end of the study."[56]

Dr Langer said, "Over time I have come to believe less and less that biology is destiny. It is not primarily our physical selves that limit us, but rather our mind-sets about our physical limits... We must ask ourselves if any of the limits we perceive as real do exist."

* * * *

At the end of this book is a list of recommended reading, books and some websites that will help you understand more about checking how we think, and how to "clear your engine for maximum forward thrust" for take-off. But the good news is that change *is* possible, because once we have asked Christ into our hearts, an inward transformation begins. It is not just an outward conforming to a set of intellectual beliefs. The Holy Spirit comes to dwell in us and He begins a process of renewal that the Bible calls a transformation. The plan that God has for our lives creates inward change.

It is quite amazing. "It blows your mind," as a friend is fond of saying. Knowing that we couldn't possibly do it ourselves, soaked in sin as we are, God decided that to make us like Jesus He had to dwell in us and do it Himself. Even then, we have choice. We can choose to listen to the Holy Spirit, or quench Him (1 Thessalonians 5:19.)

It was intriguing to read about a newly published book called *Age is Just a Number*. It was written by retired dental surgeon 97-year-old Charles Eugster to help others improve their physical health and well-being. At the age of 63 he took up rowing again and at the age of 95 he started sprinting for the first time in his life, becoming World Champion at 200m indoors and 400m outdoors. He is a world-record holder for his age group in a number of sports, and has 40 gold medals for World Masters Rowing. At the age of 89 he took advice from an Austrian former national gymnast who told him, "Your bottom, Charles, is a catastrophe!" "Can you save it?" he asked. "From that moment until the present day, Sylvia has never told me anything is impossible, and so we set to work," he said.[57] The article carried a picture of him running on the track at the British Masters in Birmingham in 2015, at the age of 96. Mr Eugster has purpose in life.

One of my daughters-in-law is a keep-fit fanatic. She exercises fiercely, cycling up mountains and running up flights of hospital steps (she is a doctor). She is tall and beautiful, with long legs. Walking alongside her, taking three steps to her one loping stride, I feel like a Pekingese alongside an Afghan hound. During one of my visits she looked at me and said, "You could run a marathon!" adding, "With practice." It was one of those rare occasions when I was lost for words. She is a determined lady and I felt slightly relieved that I was flying back home a few days later. This is not to decry running as a form of exercise – it's about finding a physical activity that you like. I go to the gym, but my colleague Janet tried it and didn't like it at all; she prefers line dancing.

Life itself is described as a race in 1 Corinthians 9:24–27. Paul was speaking metaphorically when he urged his readers to run every step with purpose, yet he also mentioned that he disciplined his body. "Run to win!" he said. In this chapter we've looked at the health of our minds and their effects on our bodies and our souls, and in the next chapter we'll see how best to look after our "earthly tents", our bodies, and a few other practical things we can be doing.

Chapter 7
Your Pre-boarding Check

Waiting in the boarding area at an airport can be the most tedious part of the journey. Before a plane takes off it's checked by engineers and by cabin crew. Then, once on board, the pilots go through a checklist that is so thorough, and so elegantly simple and easy to follow, that it was an inspiration for American surgeon Atul Gawande and his team when drawing up a pre-surgery protocol for the World Health Organization. Gawande's research took them into the airline industry, into huge skyscraper-building projects in the States, and into different hospitals around the world. They found that checklists "seem able to defend anyone, even the experienced, against failure in more tasks than we realized".[58]

While it was being constructed in the mid-1970s, a single missed communication put the iconic Citicorp building in Manhattan at risk of collapsing in a strong wind storm, and strong wind storms are not unknown in New York. The giant braces at the base of the building were designed to be joint-welded, but welding is more labour-intensive and expensive than bolting and the steel construction company decided to use bolts instead of welds. They calculated that the bolts would be strong enough – but they did not check with the structural engineer, Professor William LeMessurier. The anomaly was discovered after the building had been open for a year by an undergraduate student researching for her thesis. The building was by then fully occupied and "that summer, as Hurricane Bella made its way towards the city, an emergency crew worked at night under veil of secrecy to weld two-inch thick steel plates around the two hundred critical bolts and the building was secured".[59]

Checkpoints are important. Waiting at boarding gates with nothing much else to do, I've watched how people check that they have their essential items – passports, boarding passes, wallets, and so on. Women tend to check their bags and men tend to check their pockets – they pat themselves down. So, to make sure we have everything in place before we take off, in this chapter we'll give ourselves a gentle pat-down. If, at the end, we can say we have checked that everything is in place, we'll be ready for the rest of our journey – to become the elders that God intended from the beginning.

Is it well with your soul?

There used to be an older Welsh man in my church years ago who, after he'd received the answer to the polite, "How are you?" would ask, meaningfully, "But how is it with your soul?" At first I was taken aback, but I learned to respond with, "Yes, it is well with my soul." His enquiry was genuine, because he would pray faithfully if you mentioned a need. But underneath his question was a principle as important for your spiritual well-being as the braces were to the Citicorp building.

An expert in religious law, a Pharisee, once asked Jesus what was the most important commandment given by Moses. He was asking, in effect, what was the anchor of the faith. Jesus told him:

You must love the Lord your God with all your heart,
all your soul, and all your mind. This is the first and
greatest commandment.

A second is equally important: "Love your
neighbour as yourself." The entire law and all the
demands of the prophets are based on these two
commandments.

(Matthew 22:35–40)

Testing your bolts

Someone I knew who had come to faith late in life was an engineering type who thought in terms of "outputs", or results. Bill liked to see things that worked when put into practice. His Bible reading one day included Matthew 22, and he put the Bible down to ponder on it. As he did so, he asked the Lord, "How can I tell if I love You?" and as clear as daylight the answer came into his mind: "When you love your brothers." Bill didn't yet know the Bible well enough to know the reference in John 13:35 (NASB), "By this all men will know that you are My disciples, if you have love for one another".

It seems to be a kind of litmus test: how we love the family of God indicates how much we love our Father. Often we feel closer to other believers than we do to our natural family. It's as though the presence of the Holy Spirit in believers acts like a magnet that draws them together, crossing boundaries of social class and race. This was very evident when I lived in the Arab Gulf. Before 1971 it had been a British Protectorate, and I reckon that the expat community in the 1970s was about

100,000. As I looked around, it seemed that every nationality in the world was represented and there were clusters of Christians in all of them. Whatever our race, many of us often felt closer to each other than to our own countries' expatriates. I remember worshipping with a group of Indian Christians, sitting on a rush mat and "tarrying"; on other occasions singing songs in Arabic. In Guadalajara, Mexico, I was completely at home with my landlady, Marta (who taught me Spanish with a Sinaloa accent), and her three daughters, and everyone in our Spanish-speaking church. We shared a passion for Mexican Christian Marcos Witt's music: he wrote one of the best worship songs in the world, called simply "Gracias señor, gracias mi señor Jesus". You can hear it on YouTube at https://www.youtube.com/watch?v=uENYvCCeYXk

If you've read Canon Andrew White's *Faith Under Fire*,[60] you can't help but feel the love he has for Jesus and for believers in the Middle East. The book was written some years ago and he is no longer in Iraq, but his work of reconciliation in the region continues. *Faith Under Fire* is one of the most faith-building books I have ever read. And Andrew is exactly as the book shows him to be. I met him briefly at the Christian Resources Exhibition in Sandown, Esher, the year his book won the Christian Book of the Year award. The condition he suffers from, multiple sclerosis, has weakened him physically but inwardly he goes from strength to strength.

You may be thinking, at this point, that it's not easy to love all of God's people. Ephesians 2:22 (ESV) says, "In him you also are being built together into a dwelling place for God by the Spirit," and if you visualize this "building" as a temple and believers as stones in the walls, you can see how some would fit better at some points than others. Jesus' second commandment is so important that occasionally you have to "behave as if", or, as the Bible says, "put on love", until it grows. When we moved from one church to another as we relocated in the Arab Gulf I encountered a woman to whom I took an instant dislike: a rare experience for me. But I determined that I would behave "as if", and after a while grew fond of her. When their contract came to an end a couple of years later, at their leaving party I said how much I would miss her. She said she would miss me, too, adding, "And at first I didn't like you at all!"

I know many Christians who say they love the Lord but don't have regular fellowship because they've experienced difficulties with people at church. Often it's because of an inability within themselves to be comfortable with others or to relate to them. Were we to search more deeply we'd find hidden reasons such as a fear of rejection or, as an evangelist friend with a healing ministry suspects, an orphan spirit. But they are missing so much: the sense of belonging, of having people pray, and most of all the corporate worship, which has a special anointing. In some of our talks we ask what people would miss if they couldn't go to church, and very often they tell us it would be the "corporate worship". Fellowship also prevents us from becoming "stagnant in spirit" (Zephaniah 1:12, NASB).

Even so, God knows those who belong to Him and He always keeps hold of them (2 Timothy 2:19). Carol came to know Jesus when I lived near her in Cambridge. She's a reserved, self-contained lady with only a few friends. At first she tried attending the local churches, even staying in one for almost a year. It helped that it ran a social work project among homeless people, which she was passionate about. Then I left Cambridge and the years passed, and we always had the sort of relationship that doesn't fray, even if we didn't speak for a year or so. But whenever we made contact I felt she was slipping away from God. She had no contact with other local Christians, and once or twice seemed to be going in another direction altogether.

We hadn't spoken for almost a year when the Lord prompted her to telephone me. Carol loves caring for older people (she's a trained carer) and wanted to tell me about an elderly lady she'd cared for in her own home, who had died recently but not before Carol had led her to the Lord. She was, as the saying goes, "full of it!" Later in the conversation I said that I'd often been concerned about her, but in her inimitable Cambridge drawl she said that no, she was no good at the church thing, but she talked to the Lord and He talked to her and they were "alright". First thing in the morning, weather permitting, she sits with Him on her back doorstep looking over her big garden. She talks to Him throughout the day, giving Him all her concerns and being thankful. As wavering as she might seem to others, she is anchored to the Rock.

So may I suggest that our first "pat-down checkpoint" is how rooted we are in our faith, how we show the love of God, first to His people, and then to others? Galatians 6:10 tells us to do good, *especially* to the household of faith. If we can say, yes, we do, then it's the equivalent of having our foundation bolts firmly welded to the Rock. We may be battered by big wind storms, but we won't fall apart.

You are here on purpose, by divine design

The second pat-down point is to check that you have underlined in your mind the fact that God did not make a mistake when He designed old age. Old people are His seniors and they are here on purpose. To repeat an important point made earlier: the Lord designed it that way so that we would mature and become "ripe", emotionally and spiritually. Ripe fruit yields more juice, contains more nutrients, and is usually sweeter. The Amplified Bible says, "[Growing in grace] they will still thrive *and* bear fruit *and* prosper in old age; they will flourish *and* be vital and fresh [rich in trust and love and contentment]" (Psalm 92).

It's interesting to see how the fruit of the Spirit, noted by Paul in his letter to the Galatians – "love, joy, peace, forbearance, kindness, goodness, faithfulness, gentleness and self-control" – (Galatians 5: 22–26) is also noted in seniors by secular psychologists. It was Dr Laura Carstensen, Professor of Psychology at Stanford University, who said, "Older people are more positive in their outlook and less inclined to negativity, have increased knowledge and expertise, are more given to reconciliation than confrontation, and have better-balanced emotional lives.

The distinct attributes of older people were highlighted by two musical virtuosos, who were protesting at a proposed move to displace older people from their audiences, in favour of younger audiences. Violinist Nicola Beneditti became famous as a teenager, and was once BBC young musician of the year. Now, aged 29, she is outraged at suggestions that the organisers of symphony concerts should try to attract younger crowds at the expense of older devotees. Older people make the best audiences, she declared. "Symphony performances are suited to an atmosphere of formality and respectful attentiveness, because there's an intensity to the music itself – and the fact that it's not amplified means it's of a certain volume that requires a collective focus. I think that's an amazing thing." She's not a fan of making everything as casual as possible to attract younger people (*The Times*, June 29, 2017). Classical pianist, composer and writer Stephen Hough agrees, "With old age comes wisdom, patient, subtlety, contemplation," he said, "all qualities needed to appreciate great and complex music."

The debate began in 2016 when a festival director said that it was essential to attract younger concertgoers because there will be no one to replace the older ones as they pass on. There's a sense of déjà vu about this reasoning. Some churches have changed their music in order to attract the young, and have lost older members as a result, whereas the wiser ones are encouraging a mix of all generations. In addition, the older ones are not passing on as early as they used to, and tastes in music, as in everything else, change as we develop and mature. You don't see many over 50s in McDonalds, for instance.

Study after study shows that older people are happier than middle-aged or younger people. Older people do not take unnecessary risks."[61] It's worth remembering, too, psychologist James Hillman's insight:

> ... let us entertain the idea that character requires
> the additional years and that the long last of life is
> forced upon us neither by genes nor by conservational
> medicine nor by societal collusion. The last years
> conform and fulfil character.[62]

As the older lady riding back with me on the bus to our village said, you become more of who you are as you grow older. Yielding to the Holy Spirit, we can develop the fruit Paul describes. But if we refuse to listen to His gentle nudges we can become difficult in old age. Roger Hitchings has worked with older people for many years, including in a pastoral role, and he warns against the sins of old age, which he describes as: constantly looking back and complaining that the old days were better, self-centredness, self-indulgence, self-pity, impatience, a sense of entitlement, and spiritual apathy. But I have to say that in my years working for the Pilgrims' Friend Society, I've found more of the positive attributes among older believers than the negative. Perhaps the reason God has built a propensity for self-discovery into old age is to allow us to deal with these things so that we can enjoy Him more, and get ready for our Great Day.

After listening to a seminar entitled "Engaging and Empowering Older People", a man asked, with a sigh, "Why are older people so stubborn?" Older people can have inflexible thinking, which makes them appear to be stubborn, or they may simply be exerting their autonomy and wanting to make their own choices, especially if they feel they are being pressurized. As I began to answer, I felt God whisper into my mind that He could ask the same question of most of us, at any age. Most of us know what we *ought* to be doing but we often need a little prodding, or admonishing, from the Holy Spirit.

Are you carrying old, unwanted baggage?

The third pat-down point is to check whether you are carrying unnecessary baggage. Often, when talking about their age, people will say that they may be 50, or 60, or whatever, but they still feel the same inside as when they were younger. And in part they're correct, because the younger "us" still lives in the older "us". Think of Russian dolls; there can be over a dozen smaller dolls inside the main one. We don't suddenly start life anew at different ages and become someone else, and, as we progress from one age to another, still inside are the core beliefs and patterns of thinking and feeling we've developed over the years, including those important early, formative ones.

Someone I know in her late 80s had always kept the windows in her house firmly locked. Even in the hottest summer she could only be persuaded to open her bathroom transom window. She could always give you good reasons, such as keeping out road traffic noise or fumes. But when she moved to a second-storey room overlooking the garden in a tall-ceilinged care home, in order to seem sensible she had to change her reasons. At first it was because a cat could get in and startle her, or squirrels from the trees. Carers pointed out that even though cats are good climbers, they can't scale sheer walls, and that the nearest tree branch was at least 20 feet away and they hadn't seen a squirrel for years. So then she said she couldn't cope with butterflies or insects flying in. She would only allow a window to be opened if visitors said they would have to leave because the room was unbearably hot and airless.

Now she's in a nursing home where the bedroom's transom windows can be left open but secured, and her fear has transferred to being left on her own in the sitting room in the evening as others are taken to bed before her.

"What's the worst thing that could happen?" I asked.

"Someone could come in and frighten me," she answered. I pointed out that it is a room well inside the home, with carers moving in and out, and asked how likely that is to happen.

"I don't know, but it *could*," she replied. You don't have to be a psychotherapist to recognize that an irrational fear such as this originated in a life event, which might be even a repeated "threat" story, not even a real event, that hasn't been addressed. In his book *And Still the Music Played*, Graham Stokes, Clinical Director of BUPA, an organization with a number of care and nursing homes, tells several stories of residents whose "difficult" behaviour sprang from beliefs laid down in childhood.[63]

There can also be baggage from the past, in the form of resentment, hostility, or lack of forgiveness. I've heard some sad, even terrible, histories that have not only left scars but have influenced the development of the person, and sometimes continue to influence. This isn't a book about counselling, so it isn't the place to go into ways of dealing with these, except to recommend one of the best books I've ever encountered that can help you deal with it. *Making Peace with Your Past* takes you, step by step, through understanding issues in your past and dealing with them. The author, Professor H. Norman Wright, is an experienced Christian counsellor and psychologist, as well as Research Professor of Christian Education at Talbot School of Theology. You can read more about him at www.hnormanwright. com/index.php?main_page=page&id=15&chapter=0.

And who, looking back, doesn't regret making mistakes? Our peace comes from knowing that God has taken even these into account in His amazing planning. Romans 8:28 (CJB) says, "We know that God causes everything to work together for the good of those who love God and are called in accordance with his purpose." We may drop stitches, but God picks them up and weaves them into the pattern of our lives.

Moving from doing to being

It's important to identify beliefs about ourselves that help and ones that don't, because we become more reflective as we age. The human life cycle moves us from a state of *being,* as a child, to *doing* as an adult, and to *being-doing* as a senior, and there is a continuing process of self-discovery that reveals previously hidden aspects of the self, both good and bad.[64] This is part of God's life design too, as it leads us into reflecting more on Him and developing our relationship with Him. And it's good to look back and recall all that He's meant to us over the years: the circumstances He's touched, the tough times He's brought us through, the blessings, and, most of all, how much more we've come to learn about Him.

Being able to "just be" is a blessing in itself. Something that's often mentioned in counselling and psychology is "mindfulness", the ability to just be in the moment, focusing on the "now". If you have a mind like mine that leaps around like a cat with hot paws, being mindful doesn't come naturally, but once you've learned how to do it, it is a blessing. It soothes and refreshes.

"Just being" is one of the reasons older people and children like being with each other, says William Thomas. Visiting a nursing home that also housed a child day-care centre, he found a group of seniors and children painting flowerpots. One of the adult overseers decided it was time to move on to the next activity, and all the children trooped out of the room except one little lad, who was curled up on a senior's lap. He said that he wanted to be with Frank. "The time they were spending together soothed them both. But the adults pried the boy gently from the elder's lap, and sent him scurrying on to the next scheduled event."[65] We see this in our homes, too; a manager told me how she arranged a low table with crayons and paper for small visitors and all the residents enjoyed them being there, not just their relatives.

Moving from *doing* to *being* can be hard for some, especially those who've been particularly active in their work and are uncomfortable with introspection. Although it happens to all of us, men usually seem to find it tougher than women. An example was Ruth: one of our longest-serving care home managers, who was much loved. A nurse and midwife, she was stationed in a hospital on the south coast during the Second World War, and had traumatic memories of soldiers who had escaped Dunkirk and of some of the German airmen whose planes were shot down over the coast. She began working for Pilgrims' Friend Society in 1966, in the Hornsey Rise Home in London. It was a large home, with around 100 elderly residents. When it had to be closed for various reasons, and her residents were all moved to other Pilgrims' homes, the doctor in charge warned her to expect deaths among her charges, because some were so frail. She would have none of it. She was indomitable. She mobilized dozens of people to pray, arranged a fleet of vehicles, and transferred every one, and there was not a single death until two years after the move.

In her late 80s she was diagnosed with terminal cancer and told her pastor, "Don't you go praying for me to get better! You pray for me to go quickly!" She was known for being forthright, and I can almost feel her looking over my shoulder and saying, "Here! Watch what you are writing about me. Don't you go making me out to be some kind of special person!" Before her funeral service in 2009, her pastor asked his wife if she could think of a Bible verse that summed up Ruth. Within seconds they both thought of 2 Timothy 1:7: "For God did not give us a spirit of timidity, but a spirit of power, of love and of self-discipline." Her pastor said, "She was willing to share the gospel with anyone who would listen. We organized a charity pampering evening, to which any lady could come. To everyone's surprise, there in the car park waiting for it to begin was Ruth. She did everything – the head massage, manicure, pedicure – the lot, the whole time talking, making friends, building bridges over which she would seek to carry the good news of Jesus Christ."

A few months before she died I visited her again. She was her usual, lively self except when she asked some disturbing questions. She had been thinking, she said, about things she hadn't done that she ought to have, and things she'd done that she'd shouldn't have. "Thinking about past sins?" I checked. She nodded. "But doesn't it say that the blood of Jesus Christ cleanses us from all sin?" I asked her. She agreed, and all seemed to be well. I once read an article in a Christian magazine that said that older Christians become ever stronger in their faith as they age, but it isn't always true, partly because of the self-discovery already described and also because of increased frailty. As you begin to lose trust in your abilities you lose trust in your other "givens", too. One of our PFS supporters, a pastor who used to be a missionary, says that Satan reserves his fiercest attacks for God's older saints. I once wrote an article about frail, elderly Christians needing more of the Lord in old age, not less, and a wealthy Christian couple were so glad the point had been made that they donated acres of land to our charity.

To sum up: be prepared to move from doing, to doing-being, then to being-and-a-little-less doing, and discard any emotional baggage than can prevent you from fulfilling God's purpose for your life.

Nurture your friends

The fourth pat-down point is to do with your fellow travellers. Writing to a friend, C. S. Lewis said that friendship is the greatest of worldly "goods": "Certainly to me it is the chief happiness of life. If I had to give a piece of advice to a young man about a place to live, I think I should say, 'sacrifice almost everything to live where you can be near your friends.'"[66] Lewis said that he was very fortunate, but even so it would make a great difference if the person he was writing to, and one or two others, lived in Oxford (near him). Aristotle said, "In poverty and other misfortunes of life, true friends are a sure refuge." Amen to that! More than one person has told me that they are married to their best friend. A particular poignancy in *Dementia: Frank and Linda's Story*, a true story of a long-married couple where the husband developed dementia, was that they had been best friends since childhood. When Frank died, Linda said she had lost her best friend. One of the most moving stories in the Old Testament is the friendship between Jonathan and David (1 Samuel). It lasted even after Jonathan's death, when David brought his son, Mephibosheth, from Lo-debar and made him part of his own household. Friends are vital in our lives.

Books have been written about friendship, researchers study it, and we know that to stay psychologically healthy we need friends. Yet the challenge for seniors is staying connected. Friends move away for work or for other reasons, or are called Home. Happily, today's technology means it's easier than ever to stay in touch. Waiting for the contract for my new phone to print out, I watched as three men came into the shop and started looking at digital tablets. They all had similar features and were obviously three generations – grandfather, father, and grandson. They explained to the manager that they were looking for a tablet that Granddad could use to "hang out" with his friends and relatives abroad; something not too complicated. There's a feature or app (application) called "Hang Out" that is very easy to set up and use, and probably a dozen others out there – most people have heard of Skype. (But, looking at the interaction between the three men, I thought that Granddad was unlikely to find himself lonely anyway.) If you haven't already, learn to love the technology. Age UK offer a "set-up" programme called "Breezier" that makes managing a tablet easier for older people, with good access for relatives. You can even make new friends. I was intrigued when a woman called Louise Morse popped up on Facebook. She lives in Texas, and invited me to visit. How delightful is that?!

Friends will always be there to support you. They will listen, encourage, agree with you, affirm you, empathize, do things for you, and generally be there for you. Many major life transitions involve loosening relationships, but keeping in touch with friends prevents what has fast become the scourge of old age – loneliness. It is a big issue.

Avoiding loneliness

Last year we wrote to nearly 300 churches in a South Wales region with a list of topics they would like to see addressed at a conference we were arranging. Top of the list was loneliness. The saddest thing is that it is affecting older people particularly badly. The British Red Cross also did a survey, showing that a fifth of the adult population are either always, or often, lonely.[67]

Feelings of loneliness are more harmful to your health than 15 cigarettes a day, said researchers at Brigham Young University in Utah, echoing over a hundred different studies citing similar damaging effects. Brigham Young's study head, Dr Julianne Holt-Lunstad, said friends and family influenced health for the better by offering a "calming touch" or by helping people find meaning in their lives. "When someone is connected to a group and feels responsibility for other people, that sense of purpose and meaning translates to taking better care of themselves and taking fewer risks," she said.[68]

Dr Robert Wilson is senior neuropsychologist of the Rush Alzheimer's Disease Center, Chicago. His team published findings showing that the risk of developing Alzheimer's disease increased approximately 51 per cent for each point on a loneliness scale, so that a person with a high loneliness score (3.2) had about a 2.1 times greater risk of developing Alzheimer's disease than a person with a low score (1.4). The findings did not change significantly when the researchers factored in markers of social isolation, such as a small network and infrequent social activities.[69] "Humans are very social creatures. We need healthy interactions with others to maintain our health," he said.

Some time ago the manager of a local superstore told me that their security cameras regularly spot an older person picking up and eating a bar of chocolate without paying for it, but staff are instructed to ignore it. He said they knew the pensioners came into the store in the first place because it was warm and they couldn't afford proper heating at home. This store is not in the wealthiest part of town, and we were speaking in wintertime.

Recently, charity Age UK found that 600,000 older people are relying on shopping trips to beat loneliness: they would have no one to talk to if they didn't visit the supermarket. Age UK is encouraging supermarket staff to chat with an older person, saying how it can brighten up their day and do more good than most of us would ever guess. The University of Hertfordshire recommended that supermarkets set up a slow-lane checkout for isolated pensioners, so they would have time to chat.

Deryn van der Tang is manager of our retirement housing in Bedford. She has moved across cities and continents more than once, including travelling on her own to destinations where she didn't speak the language. She said, "When you are in a time of transition, that is crossing the bridge from one place or lifestyle into another, you must expect to go through a period of loneliness while you pick up the pieces of your life again. Knowing who you really are in Christ and the gifts He has given you are the foundation to finding your way. This is the time to really deepen your relationship with God, to be more in tune with His voice and leading. In these times of transition, I have always found God to be close and directing me, putting people in my path, or giving me a *rhema* out of His Word. When I look back on these times my faith has deepened greatly, as I know that if He has led and provided for me in the past He will do so in the future."

The important thing about loneliness is to recognize it and take steps to avoid it now. We can encourage different interest groups at church, join social activities such as book clubs, and, looking around, find many other things we can not only do but be a blessing in.

A final note on this topic is that feelings of loneliness in older people can take the form of a low-level grieving, like a dull but nagging toothache, even years after a spouse has died. A 95-year-old interviewed on radio told how he had "lovely people in his life" and had spent Christmas with his daughter, but his wife and he had always seen the New Year in together and she had died four years earlier. "Oh, the loneliness," he said.

A sense of fulfilment and gratitude

The fifth pat-down point is about building a sense of fulfilment and gratitude; of having the important things done, or dealt with. Emma, the manager of one of our care homes in Plymouth, organized a special "Hopes and Dreams" event for residents and their relatives. After a clotted cream tea (they're in Devon, after all!), they were encouraged to talk about their hopes and dreams, no matter how trivial or fanciful they felt them to be, and were given cloud-shaped pieces of white paper to write them down on. The clouds were then pinned to a clothes line and stretched across the lounge's blue-painted wall, which, incidentally, matches the colour of the sky outside on a good day.

A resident wrote that she would love to see an old film she'd enjoyed years ago, and staff were able to find a DVD of it and play it for her; the others enjoyed it too. Another said she would love to visit her daughter who lives overseas, and, although she is too frail to travel, thanks to Google Earth a carer was able to "fly" her to the country, then to the region, then to her daughter's house. It was a very meaningful trip for her. Everyone found the experience to be overwhelmingly positive, said Emma, and she plans to hold it twice a year.

If we have dreams and hopes, why not see if we can fulfil them as much as we can now? Also, why not write down the things we've already achieved in our lives, and thank God for them? If you think this sounds boastful, consider Isaiah 26:12, where Isaiah noted, "Lord, you will grant us peace; all we have accomplished is really from you" (NLT). It's an echo of Philippians 2:13 (NASB), which says, "For it is God who is at work in you, both to will and to work for *His* good pleasure." Try it! Gratefulness increases our sense of well-being, but, more importantly, it honours God. A little warning here: one of our negative biases is that we feel we haven't achieved much at all. An example of this was Patrick, a computer programmer struggling with a new regime at work. While under this stress he began to believe that he was no good and that he'd never been any good. Writing out a list of the programmes he'd completed over the years rebalanced his thinking. He'd written thousands of lines of computer code. It helps to ask the Holy Spirit to bring things to your memory. The encouraging thing is that there will be things you did, little touches of encouragement or practical help that you will have forgotten, but, like thrown stones rippling through water, they're still having an effect.

Looking after your earthly tent

Our physical well-being is our sixth pat-down point. There can be few people in the developed world who do not know what we ought to be doing to stay physically healthy. We are bombarded with instructions on all media platforms. To summarize the main guidelines: they are to a) eat a healthy diet – the Mediterranean diet is the most promoted; b) do exercise, such as walking for 30 minutes five times a week; c) watch your blood pressure (even skinny people can have high blood pressure); d) get enough sleep; e) avoid smoking; f) be careful to maintain good posture. Although it doesn't happen to everyone, many people become bowed over as they age, and it doesn't help with walking well. Sticking to these guidelines has quite startling results, as the findings of one of the world's longest-running epidemiology studies, the Caerphilly Study, demonstrated. And findings by Loughborough University and others showed that even low levels of exercise can make a difference; as little as two 30-minute walks twice a week have a significant effect.

The Caerphilly Study began in 1979, when 2,500 men were enrolled and asked to follow five simple rules – eat sensibly, exercise, drink less, keep their weight down, and never smoke. Only 25 managed to stick to the plan, but now, 35 years later, they are far fitter and healthier than those who gave up. The men who stuck to four or five of the healthy behaviours during the 30 years of follow-up experienced on average a 73 per cent reduction in diabetes, a 67 per cent reduction in vascular disease, a 35 per cent reduction in cancer (purely attributable to not smoking), and a 64 per cent reduction in cognitive impairment and dementia. Also, the Caerphilly area is known for its good social cohesion.

Learning and staying engaged

The seventh and last pat-down point is about learning and staying engaged. *"Be the most interesting person you know, subscribe to Live Science,"* says their website. It made me smile but it does have a point, as research is showing more and more the importance of learning. It increases the number of synapses – the points of connection between the neurons in your brain, especially if it involves complex concepts. Every new thought you have creates new connections between your neurons, and complex thoughts create complex connections. The effects of education are seen in dementia rates, with fewer cases among those with higher education levels. But while some brain-training games are helpful, your brain really sparks with social activities.

Why not join an evening class? Gill, a 77-year-old, is learning Welsh at night school, an activity so complex it will surely protect her brain for years. (The Welsh language uses the same alphabet as the English, but uses the letters differently, often allocating different sounds to them. A student observed that it's as though the Welsh were handed the English alphabet and told to "see what you can do with this".) Gill is doing it to be able to converse with her grandson; a lovely example of purpose, persistence, and social motivation.

There is a gem of a story in Genesis 47:7–10: "Then Joseph brought in his father, Jacob, and presented him to Pharaoh. And

Jacob blessed Pharaoh. 'How old are you?' Pharaoh asked him. Jacob replied, 'I have travelled this earth for 130 hard years. But my life has been short compared to the lives of my ancestors.' Then Jacob blessed Pharaoh again before leaving his court." As ruler of Egypt, Pharaoh had immense power, but he recognized the wisdom and spiritual standing of the old patriarch and accepted his blessing. In this he was wiser than Solomon's son, Rehoboam, who "rejected the advice of the older men and instead asked the opinion of the young men who had grown up with him and were now his advisers" (1 Kings 12:8, NLT). The result was national disaster and civil war.[70] In contrast, Egypt, ruled by Joseph's Pharaoh, prospered.

Chapter 8
Elderhood – Seniors with Purpose

"You won't believe it! We get less grumpy with age!"[71] was the headline in the press about research newly published by Cambridge University, which showed that physical changes in the brain as we age mean that we become less neurotic and more agreeable.[72] Perhaps it means that the grumpy old man is simply the grumpy young man with years added. It would also seem to mean that the physical changes are a tiny part of God's plan to prepare His seniors for elderhood; another little proof, perhaps, that when it comes to God's working His purpose out age has *everything* to do with it.

While there are things that would help at any age, for instance, inviting the Holy Spirit to renew our thoughts and attitudes (Ephesians 4:23), this book looks at the sweep of age from after retirement until we're called Home. Even there we won't be lolling about with our feet up. Author Randy Alcorn says there will be work for us to do in heaven, because "God Himself is a worker. He didn't create the world and then retire." Jesus said, "My Father is always at his work to this very day, and I, too, am working" (John 5:17, NIV).[73]

Our jobs give us a sense of accomplishment and purpose, and in our culture they can be a kind of shorthand for defining who we are: "I'm a teacher", or "I'm a plumber", and so on.

Many military people keep their titles after retirement, which seems to be a mark of respect for the important role they played for their country. Doctors do the same, and also, I believe, professors. To a great extent our characters are moulded by our work. An editor is always an editor, spotting missing links in narrative whether spoken or written. A nurse is always a nurse, noticing symptoms sometimes before the person knows they have them. And a teacher is always a teacher – and children seem to recognize that, too, although for them there's no post-retirement recognition. When we step down from work it can affect our sense of identity, and how we and others "frame" ourselves. However, God has prepared a role for seniors, and it is called "elderhood". There is work to be done.

Initially, many people say they are busier after retirement than before, and wonder how they ever managed to fit in a working life. They don't seem to have time to ask themselves, "What's my purpose in life?" But others feel discombobulated. I once asked an audience of around 100 people in their 70s and 80s to raise their hands if they were glad they'd retired. Half the hands went up. The others missed their jobs; the social connections, the sense of accomplishment and, often, the identity that their jobs gave them. Some said they didn't feel they were being useful any more, rather like the 87-year-old who said he didn't see why his doctors had helped him to stay alive.

One of our seminars is called "Developing Usefulness in Old Age". Again, with a relatively small group we were able to discuss what being useful meant to them. How did they see it? They were silent for quite a few minutes, and then one ventured, "Helping with the teas and coffees in church." After a few more minutes another said, "Helping other people." Our definition of "being useful" is not something that we think about very often. For most of our life we haven't had the time to consider whether or not we were useful; indeed, there were times when we felt that we were being far *too* useful. For years we juggled commitments, sliced time, neglected ourselves, and wished there were more hours in the day. We didn't need to enquire about our purpose in life because it was constantly hurling itself at us.

We are not looking at the utilitarian view of human beings, the one that says that unless people are doing something with a defined result, they are no longer of any use. God's "usefulness" is enshrined in the two commandments that Jesus said are the most important of all. When we are embracing the first, the second is a natural outflow.

The key to our purpose

So now here we are: seniors buckled into the Scriptures, knowing that we are here by design, equipped by God to do what He's planned for us in advance, and with more time than we ever thought existed, asking ourselves – what now? Where do we go from here?

The key is in Ephesians 2:10, which says, "For we are His workmanship, created in Christ Jesus for good works, which God prepared beforehand so that we would walk in them" (NASB). The Complete Jewish Bible puts it like this: "For we are of God's making, created in union with the Messiah Yeshua for a life of good actions already prepared by God for us to do."

It couldn't be clearer. God has all our "good actions" planned in advance. Furthermore, He has equipped us with the skills to do them – talents that are often evident in childhood. One of my sons used to dismantle anything he could get his hands on, including the clock on his bedroom wall. Now he installs and maintains huge vacuum furnaces with all their electronic and computerized controls. After I'd mentioned this "equipping" in a talk, a woman told me how her daughter used to take her dolls apart when she was very young, and now she's a surgeon.

Charles Haddon Spurgeon was a famous 19th-century preacher. From time to time he would preach a sermon on behalf of The Aged Pilgrims' Friend Society, which was the original name of our charity. On one memorable occasion his address followed a talk by a trustee who, after describing the work, suggested that people in the congregation might consider leaving a legacy to the Society in their will. Spurgeon was far more forthright, saying it would be better for people who had any money to donate it now, rather than waiting until they died.

He also preached on God's plan for our lives. In a sermon at the Metropolitan Tabernacle in London he said, "Not only are we ourselves in the hand of the Lord, but all that surrounds us. Our times make up a kind of atmosphere of existence; and all this is under divine arrangement. We dwell within the palm of God's hand. We are absolutely at His disposal, and all our circumstances are arranged by Him in all their details. We are comforted to have it so."[74]

"All our circumstances are arranged by Him in all their details" is another confirmation that we don't have to worry about needing to look for our "good works", because His plan will bring them to us. "The Lord directs our steps, so why try to understand everything along the way?" asks Proverbs 20:24.

Sometimes the skills themselves draw people into the "works" (Proverbs 18:16.) For example, people who've worked in banking often find themselves doing the church's accounts, and helping those in the fellowship who are not good at budgeting and managing money. A retired master baker makes cakes for charity events, and an artist I know teaches screen printing in India so that people there can make a living.

In his book, *The Longevity Revolution: The Benefits and Challenges of Living a Long Life*, Robert Butler suggests that people "who have retired from the worlds of science, business, and academia, among others, could teach, mentor, and sponsor young people". He suggested setting up a registry of retired scientists who could lead after-school "enrichment programs for children, in this nation of science illiteracy". He also saw the need not to "lose the great gifts of craftsmanship and the arts carried out by older persons", and listed volunteering opportunities available in the States within a range of organizations. There are countless opportunities for volunteer work today, as reports by the RVS and Age UK show.

How can older people play a role in society?

Seniors listening to troubled teenagers helped to turn around a failing school in a disadvantaged part of England. Research from Japan and the United States showed that getting youngsters together with pensioners not only improved the schoolchildren's confidence and exam results, but also enhanced the memory and physical strength of the older participants. TV's Hairy Bikers, Si King and Dave Myers (who both struggled at school), were so inspired they set out to see if it could work in Britain.

The project matched 12 disruptive and troubled pupils aged between 13 and 15 from a school with the lowest GCSE results in the country with 12 older people. All underwent a series of psychological tests. The schoolchildren's self-esteem and confidence were measured, as were the seniors' cognitive skills and mobility.

The outcome was outstanding. Teachers said the pupils' improved self-esteem and performance had a ripple effect on other pupils and the Academy is now in the country's top-ten most improving schools. There were benefits for the older people too, with tests showing improved movement and memory, as well increased capacity for socializing. The full story can be read here: http://www.dailymail.co.uk/news/article-3613572/Magical-friendships-troubled-teenagers-link-OAPs-looking-void-lives-transformed.html

The experiment produced such good results for the students and the older people involved that grants were being sought to help roll it out across the country. Hopefully, austerity and current tight finances have not knocked it on the head. However, could it be an inspiration for churches to talk to the team and learn about the project, so their older people could provide the same listening ear for troubled pupils in their local schools?

* * * *

"How can older people play a bigger role in society?" was the headline question in a newspaper article,[75] which mentioned the qualities of older people, their skills and experience, and ways of supporting them to enable them to contribute, such as better transport, etc., but without defining what that "bigger role" could be. There seems to be no pattern in the general mind of what older people could do. It's as though we're entering uncharted territory needing new road maps, in spite of those already lit up by the "gleams of dawn" described earlier, those seniors who have shown the way.

Even in terms of economics, where figures are thrown up like the numbered balls in the TV lottery machine, few people seem to recognize the role of older people and their contributions. For example, who knows that "people aged 65 and over in the UK contributed £61bn to the economy in 2013 through employment, informal caring, and volunteering"? And that number "equals 4.6 per cent of gross value added, and is six times more than the money spent on social care by local authorities in England?"[76] According to Age UK, older people providing childcare contributed £6.6bn, and their volunteering amounted to nearly £6bn. I have never heard or seen these figures in the media.

A Boomers' benign revolution

Seniors are already playing a bigger role in society than is generally realized, and it's one that will become larger as more people become "old" – even though, as we've said earlier, the threshold for old age is shifting further and further back. However, more and more Boomers are joining the ranks of seniors every month. The hope is that, as this generation becomes ever larger, the Boomers' non-conformist attitude and sheer weight of numbers will make them as effective a crucible for change in perception as it did when they were adults. When they find that there is life on the other side of adulthood and that they have not "hurtled into an abyss of brokenness", they may change their faulty life-design concept for one closer to reality. Instead of a "malign enlargement of adulthood" they may begin to promote the qualities of "elderhood", creating a balanced view more in line with God's life design.

Writing in *Time US*, Dr Laura Carstensen said that Boomers may, indeed, spark a second revolution.[77] But this would be a quieter revolution, not the Woodstock imagined, with far less "chanting in the streets". "Instead, boomers could become an army of millions of grey-haired people, better educated than any previous generation, armed with unprecedented financial resources and decades of experience, ready to solve the practical problems of life. This revolution could finally help the nation become a better place for young people." As Marc Freedman, the CEO of Encore.org, says, "Maybe we can stop trying to stay young and instead rally to help people who actually are. Now wouldn't that be a fitting legacy for the Woodstock generation?" Instead of intergenerational war, there would be intergenerational blessing.

There can't be a better example of this type of legacy than the story of Arthur (in his 80s) and Deborah (in her 50s). They lived next door to each other for 30 years, raising families and becoming close friends. "He was a knowledgeable man with many interests," said Deborah. "He blessed me with his knowledge. He loved history and birdwatching – and he knew so much about them. We used to do the birdwatching together, looking over the nature reserve at the back of the gardens. He was like a grandfather to me." To qualify as a teacher Deborah needed a GCSE mathematics certificate, and Arthur helped her study for it, going to night school for lessons himself while

Deborah went to the local comprehensive school. They took their exams at the same time in the same classroom, sitting in the same row as Deborah's son.

Five years before he died, Arthur became ill. Deborah looked after him as much as she could. When a chest infection took him to hospital, he was told that he wasn't well enough to go back to his own home and would have to go into a care home. He hated the idea, and died in hospital. "He just gave up, I believe," said Deborah. "I felt that if only I'd been able to take care of him he would have gone back home and he would have been alright."

She decided to give up teaching and train as a carer to help other older people in similar situations. At first she worked for a domiciliary care agency, looking after older people in their own homes, but she found the time spent driving between visits worrying and distracting. So she resigned, and applied to work in our care home in Plymouth. "I feel that I've come home," she said. "I've never felt more welcome in a place of work! I've got 21 grandmas and granddads now, all different, all so interesting! Some are challenging, some very needy – needing your attention not just your care; some are quite lonely, and you as a carer take the place of that, fill those little gaps. They give you just as much back – they're thankful. Not a day goes by when we don't laugh!"

Arthur's friendship did not just bless Deborah in his lifetime, but continues to bless the home's current residents and all those who will follow. Deborah's love for older people will last a lifetime, and will inspire others, too.

* * * *

Let's look again at God's purpose for His elders. They are to tell of His goodness and faithfulness, sharing from a lifetime's experience. Psalm 71:18 is an appeal to give the writer strength so that, he tells the Lord, he can "proclaim your might to another generation, your power to all those to come" (ESV). Declaring God's goodness is at the heart of the Bible's picture of a godly older person. And, according to research published by the Evangelical Alliance, there's never been a better time to talk about faith.

Among the findings were that, in the UK, non-Christians attribute more positive than negative qualities to the Christians they know; two-thirds of practising UK Christians have talked about Jesus with a non-Christian in the past month; 39 per cent of all UK adults believe that Jesus was mythical, and not a real person; 43 per cent believe in the resurrection of Jesus Christ from the dead; a third of practising Christians feel afraid of causing offence when talking to non-Christians – but two-thirds don't; 20 per cent of those surveyed said they were open to an encounter with Jesus; 51 per cent were comfortable with being spoken to; and 42 per cent of all UK non-Christians who know a Christian have never had a conversation with them about Jesus.

Older saints are to encourage others

Encouragement is always good, but especially when it's first-hand. Deryn's Uncle Theo was still emailing friends and family at the age of 101 to encourage them. She found his philosophy about serving the Lord joyfully in difficult circumstances particularly inspiring: "At one stage, his wife, my great-aunt Elvin, had to go into nursing care with dementia and skin cancer. Uncle Theo moved into Assisted Living. It was at that time that he sent an email to a friend, which he later copied to me. It read as follows:

> 'I've experienced so many miracles in my life. That's
> why I'm still alive. When I was 44 I couldn't get any
> insurance, they said because of my medical records.
> And here I am still alive at 101 years and 5 months.
> Elvin is 97.
>
> Almost a year ago when we had to vacate our lovely
> flat and come here, I went through some awful times,
> over and above the stress of separation and moving.
> I'll spare you the details. But I actually heard the devil
> talking to me. He asked why I continue to trust God
> when He's not answering my prayers! Later on, when
> almost all those problems were overcome, I heard the
> Lord saying to me, "Yes, you did keep trusting and
> praising Me, but you did not do so joyfully." I have
> taken the hint. And despite my condition I remain
> content and joyful. I keep occupied. So I have no time
> to be bored or to get miserable.'"

* * * *

All believers are to watch and pray, but seniors usually have more time and a better grasp of what's really needed, being able to take the long view. People living in our retirement housing and in our care homes are great prayer warriors. They pray for missionaries, for their churches, for their families, for world issues, and for each other and staff at the home. Sitting alongside an elderly resident during a prayer meeting, I heard her thanking God for the friendships they enjoyed with each other in the home. "Fervent prayer availeth much", as the King James Bible puts it (James 5:16). (Sometimes the old words have more depth than the modern!) There's the story of the young pastor who knew he was held up in prayer each day by his grandma. After she died, he felt bereft, and mentioned it from the pulpit. From the congregation came a little chorus of calls from the older ladies saying, "I'll be your grandma now!"

Exodus 17:8–15 is the story of the Hebrews' battle against the Amalekites, with Joshua in charge. Moses had told him to choose some men and go out and fight, while he, Moses, held the staff of God in his hands, in other words, interceding in prayer. Moses, Aaron, and Hur climbed to the top of a nearby hill:

> As long as Moses held up the staff in his hand, the Israelites had the advantage. But whenever he dropped his hand, the Amalekites gained the advantage. Moses' arms soon became so tired he could no longer hold them up. So Aaron and Hur found a stone for him to sit on. Then they stood on each side of Moses, holding up his hands. So his hands held steady until sunset. As a result, Joshua overwhelmed the army of Amalek in battle.
>
> *(Exodus 17:11–13, NLT)*

Three seniors praying changed the course of history

Samuel understood the power of prayer. "I will certainly not sin against the Lord by ending my prayers for you. And I will continue to teach you what is good and right," he told an assembly, adding for good measure, "but be sure to fear the Lord and faithfully serve him. Think of all the wonderful things he has done for you" (1 Samuel 12:23–24). "Thinking about the wonderful things He has done for you" is very sound advice:

research shows than being grateful is physically, as well as psychologically, good for you.

We're told to never stop praying, to "pray without ceasing" (1 Thessalonians 5:17). I used to resent what I saw as unproductive time spent travelling by train from one place to another. Then I reframed it as "my time", when I could indulge in reading books, but the Lord reminded me that all my times are in His hands, so I reframed it again as "Father time". People travelling in Great Western Railway trains and on the London Underground would be surprised to know that they've been prayed for, sometimes quite intensely. But "praying without ceasing" doesn't mean always interceding; it includes keeping the Father company, thanking Him and telling Him how wonderful He is, and hearing from Him. This "reframing" works in the car, too, producing an amazingly benign frame of mind, which makes me wonder whether there are other people in the world who, because of this, don't mind being stuck in traffic hold-ups – within reason. It brings even the M25 into a Romans 8:28 context!

Seniors are "watchmen on the wall", being vigilant and speaking out against things that are wrong. (They also have more time to get involved in such actions.) For example, there will always be attempts to legalize euthanasia, driven largely by an organization that used to be known as the National Society for the Legalization of Euthanasia. The book *Right to Die?*, written by John Wyatt, a member of the Christian Medical Fellowship and Professor of Ethics and Perinatology at University College London, lays out the issues with crystal clarity, revealing the source of the movement and the belief that some lives have no value. "The supporters of the Bill use deliberately soft-sounding language such as 'assisted dying' to make it sound gentle, natural and compassionate," he says. "In reality what is proposed w[ould be] a major change in the law on intentional killing and a major change in medical practice." The campaign is no longer focused on unbearable suffering; instead, there is a rising demand for choice and control over the time and manner of death, coupled with fears about the social and economic consequences of increasing numbers of elderly and dependent individuals.

Saving money by euthanizing people who are desperately ill is top of the agenda in research published by the influential *Canadian Medical Association Journal*. Their report reached a chilling conclusion that "providing medical assistance in dying in Canada... could result in substantial savings".[78] It sounds so reasonable, hastening death for those already dying by a few weeks, but experience in Belgium shows that such a law would open the floodgates, so that patients whose quality of life was deemed to be poor by their doctors would be euthanized without their consent.

"The only thing necessary for the triumph of evil is for good men to do nothing," said Irish statesman Edmund Burke (1729–97). He also said that "nobody made a greater mistake than he who did nothing because he could do only a little". It's easy to think that the little we can do is unimportant. A lever and the right place to stand would enable Archimedes to move the world, he said. In the last attempt to legalize euthanasia in the British parliament, millions of concerned voters stood in the right place in their individual worlds and used their levers – their emails, petitions, and prayers – to move their Members of Parliament towards making the right decision. Small actions can have huge consequences.

"Good and evil both increase at compound interest," wrote C. S. Lewis; "that is why the little decisions you and I make every day are of such infinite importance. The smallest good act today is the capture of a strategic point from which, a few months later, you may be able to go on to victories you never dreamed of. An apparently trivial indulgence in lust or anger today is the loss of a ridge or railway line or bridgehead from which the enemy may launch an attack otherwise impossible."[79]

Building community

One of the small, good acts that could be more strategic than we realize is to help to support our local retailers. My Cambridge vicar and I produced a monthly magazine, which was largely funded by advertising from local retailers. He was an expert at desktop printing and I would write articles and cajole others into doing the same. It also gave me an opportunity to visit the shops in the parish, getting to know them and selling advertising space, and, sometimes, writing their stories. The magazine twice won first place in a competition for parish magazines – mainly, I'm convinced, because of the vicar's expertise, but the judges also noted their pleasure that it had involved local shops.

Local retailers work hard. They don't make a fortune, and they are so useful for older people. They're often the last bastion against the globalization that has done so much harm to communities and older people. One of the most extraordinary speeches by a governor of the Bank of England was the Roscoe Lecture given in December 2016 at John Moores University in Liverpool. I'm surprised that it hasn't been more widely reported.

"There is a growing sense of 'isolation and detachment' among people who feel left behind by globalization," said Mark Carney. He didn't mention older people in particular, but I did in my book *Dementia: Pathways to Hope*, published in 2015.[80] As well as depressing wages and devaluing skills, commercial globalization has had an even more devastating effect on older people by removing their main supports in old age – their families, who move away for work. I wrote:

> *Perhaps the most rapid change in human behaviour, and by far the most significant, is the phenomenon known as globalization. It's been happening gradually for hundreds of years but has been speeded up in the last 20 by the arrival of the internet. Our high streets are disappearing as we purchase more and more online. Local producers have become specialists, and global corporations are taking over, and the biggest companies are no longer national firms but multinational corporations with subsidiaries in many countries. Some global corporations are more powerful than national governments, with turnovers surpassing countries' GDP (gross domestic product).*
>
> *The effects were foreseen, and warned about. In a paper published in the journal* Ageing and Society,[81] *Gail Wilson, Department of Social Policy, London School of Economics and Political Science, wrote, "Free trade, economic restructuring, the globalization of finance, and the surge in migration, have in*

> *most parts of the world tended to produce harmful consequences for older people. These developments have been overseen, and sometimes dictated by inter-governmental organizations (IGOs) such as the International Monetary Fund (IMF), the World Bank, and the World Trade Organization (WTO), while other IGOs with less power have been limited to anti-ageist exhortation."*
>
> *Dr Dhrubodhi Mukherjee was a consultant with the World Bank in their Urban Renewal Program in India. He is now Assistant Professor at the School of Social Work, at Southern Illinois University. Dr Mukherjee said, "Globalization has contributed to economic wellbeing for many developing nations, but it has reduced 'family' into a non-viable economic institution for the elderly by promoting urbanized social values of individualism and atomic self-interest."*

Mr Carney noted that "many people across the advanced world were 'losing trust' in a system that did not 'raise all boats'. Far from enjoying a 'golden era', globalization... has become 'associated with low wages, insecure employment, stateless corporations, and striking inequalities'". Measures announced in the 2016 Autumn Statement, including higher investment spending, would "begin the process of rebalancing policies", and putting "individuals back in control" by equipping workers with the skills needed to adapt to technological change were vital. "The tide must be turned back on stateless corporations" to maintain a sense of fairness. "Companies must be rooted and pay tax somewhere," he said.[82]

But we can do something about it right now. We can go to our high streets and our corner shops and begin to buy locally. Many bookshops, including Christian bookshops, have been hit hard by globalization. But perhaps it requires an even more fundamental shift in our thinking. A very timely book is the Archbishop of Canterbury's new book, *Dethroning Mammon*.[83] In it he writes that "the problem with materialism… is not that it exists, but that it dominates. It shouts so loudly that it overrides our caring about other things of greater value".

The Archbishop's book shows how we have fallen under the rule of Mammon, the false God. Each one of us is only a small stone, but if we each step into the water by supporting local enterprises, together we can build a wall to form a safe harbour.

In a chapter on John Wesley the preacher as an old man, writer John Telford observed, "Wherever he went he diffused a portion of his own felicity. Easy and affable in his demeanour he accommodated himself to every sort of company, and showed how happily the most finished courtesy may be blended with the most perfect piety."[84] Wouldn't it be good if that could be said of all older people? It could be the little acts of kindness that make the biggest changes and that offer the greatest potential in elderhood.

Chapter 9
Polishing the Family Silver – Notes for Churches

Sometimes people will tell you that their faith is a very private matter, which usually means that they don't want to talk about it. It's true that our relationship with Jesus Christ is indeed very close and personal, though the Scriptures make it clear that we are not to keep our faith to ourselves – we are to tell others. We're also told not to neglect the assembling of ourselves together. We need each other's support and encouragement, not just to live, but to fulfil the role God has designed us for.

But many churches, kind as they are to their older members, have ageist attitudes. How could they not? A government health minister said that the NHS is ageist because it is full of people drawn from an ageist society, and the same can be said about us and our churches.

Not me, and not my church, you may be thinking. Let's look at a common perception that is a litmus test for how we see our seniors, and one which I believe calls for the biggest shift in attitude if we are to realize the whole of God's plan for His church. The following diagram illustrates a psychological concept called Transactional Analysis.

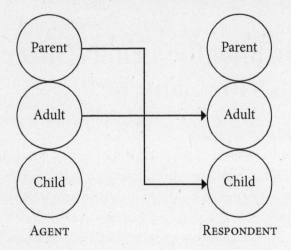

AGENT   RESPONDENT

The theory is that each person has three ego states: parent, adult, or child. The parent ego is the position of authority, with a sense of relating "top-down" to others. The child state is often on the receiving end of the "parent", reacting with emotions formed as a child. The adult state is one where parent and child are in balance, and where we relate to each other on an equal basis. Phrases such as "Oh come on, let's be adult about this!" or "You're being childish" are often heard in arguments.

When older people appear frailer, or simply because they are looking older (that is, they've left adulthood), often the parent–child transaction is evoked and the senior is seen and treated as a child. "Infantilizing" older people is one of the bugbears of being in hospital; nurses have only the best intentions of being kind, but using a patient's forename without permission, or calling them "dear", strips the person of their position as a senior. If we see people as "old dears" needing help, people who need things to be done for them, or to them, then we are thinking as parent–child. One of my friends, a very correct sort of lady, who has just collected her bus pass, commented recently that her hairdresser has just begun calling her "darling".

It's the same principle as seeing the person, not the deficits, in someone with dementia. We can have a view of older people that sees their deficits and not their characters. But if our perception of older people is that they are seniors, equipped on purpose by God for the role of elderhood in society (not the same thing as elders in church), despite their physical frailty, then we will relate as adult to adult. We will support seniors in a way that enables them to be all that God intended.

The challenge arises when seniors have so absorbed decades of ageism themselves that, all unawares, they cast themselves in the child role, and, sadly, the culture in many churches reinforces this. Very rarely do they teach about the life experiences and qualities of their seniors, or their talents. Not all churches, I hasten to add. Some pastors, especially in rural areas, acknowledge that their seniors are the ones who keep the church, including its outreach, going.

After one of our seminars, a couple of pastors asked the question, "How can we encourage our older members to become more engaged in the church?" We didn't have time to answer the question fully then, but our findings from hundreds of conversations with older people have given us an outline of the answer.

Sometimes disengagement and falling away occur because of apathy and spiritual stagnation (Zephaniah 1:12), or depression. Twenty-two per cent of older men and 28 per cent of older women suffer from depression, which can be caused by discrimination (there it is again), lack of participation in meaningful activities, difficulties with relationships, poor physical health, and poverty.

Depression can often be averted when the person is listened to with intentional, *active* listening. Counsellors have all experienced people who came for counselling and talked non-stop for most of the first session, saying afterwards that they felt better already. Among the great "lacks" in today's world is a lack of real listening. Listening is more than just hearing. It tells the person that they are worth listening to and that their concerns are real. Perhaps churches could have a seniors' "listening" circle, similar to the Hairy Bikers' social experiment, mentioned earlier.

We also found that seniors become disengaged from church when they no longer feel a sense of purpose in it. Sometimes, they've told us, it's because the focus of the church has switched to the young, and they feel completely left out and unimportant. A number of church leaders have told us that they haven't been trained in pastoring older people, and while there are many youth leaders, few churches have anything similar for older people. On the other hand, there are churches that actively engage with their seniors, and where necessary give them the support they need to do their "good works".

Putting seniors' light on a stand

The first thing is for church leaders to preach about the value of older people and their purpose in God's plan. Make it known to everyone. I'd be really interested to know how many have heard a sermon on God's purposes for older people. Also, although it might be taking it a little too far, I'd like to see Leviticus 31:19 in action, where, in Sunday services, we take a moment to "rise in the presence of the elderly". I've only seen this happen once, some years ago at a Christian weekend away in the Cotswolds. The leader wanted to acknowledge these seniors' faithfulness over the years, and that they were still "running the race". It was a simple act, but had such a sense of significance that I remember it still.

Also, "opt-out" retirement thinking has to be challenged. Seniors are not meant to become the Saga generation – they have things to do for God. One church gives its members tracts to keep in their pockets. A lady who became very poorly sighted used to sit in a bus shelter and ask a waiting person if he or she would read it to her. Then she would ask, "What do you think of that?"

Psalm 78 talks about generation after generation telling the next generation about the things that God has done. Our churches could be supporting older people in their ministry of "telling out" God's work in their lives. Think about inviting them to speak on a Sunday morning, even. A pastor told me how his congregation were riveted by the testimony of one of their seniors who told of his experience as a soldier liberating a notorious Nazi prison camp. On another occasion, another told of taking Bibles into Romania when it was under communist rule, and of the Lord's miraculous interventions. Yet another told of running a home for unmarried mothers and their babies, and helping to lead them to Christ. Seniors have reservoirs of experiences to share.

Encouraging engagement

Many churches are good at involving seniors in "helping" activities, such as Parents/Carers and Toddlers. It would be interesting to know how involved they are in decisions made by the fellowship, including the choice of worship music. Most that we've met are very happy with the new songs but see no reason for abandoning the old hymns. Why not a mixture of both? But it's about more than musical harmony... the idea is to include them in discussions. Older people won't normally put themselves forward, so it's down to the pastoral team to ask. Where they feel excluded, they will often quietly leave.

In Janet's church, she and another member have been given a kind of watching brief for their seniors. They get to know them and, if one is absent, they will telephone to ask if they are alright. Make sure names and phone numbers are in your church directory.

Thinking of the school listening project and how well that worked, it is good to encourage activities that bring younger and older members together. For example, seniors could be prayer supporters for the younger, praying for exams, relationships, and other concerns. Technology clubs are places where younger members show seniors how to "hang out" on their digital tablets and "FaceTime" and Skype on their phones, as well as helping with their laptops. Involving older and younger people in discussions will often bring up a raft of ideas.

Encourage seniors to form their own groups, if they don't already have one. In a church in Devon an original group of 30 seniors formed separate interest groups and grew in the process, inviting non-church friends along. Hold special outreach days that involve seniors too. A church in Wiltshire held a "pampering" day, to attract people from the area into church. The pampering (manicures, pedicures, head-and-neck massage, make-up) was done by a local company. As mentioned earlier, Ruth, a church member in her late 80s, went in and sampled all the pampering, building bridges with the manicurists and others, and, as the Spirit led, talking about Jesus.

Brain and Soul Boosting for Seniors

Seniors could be leading groups in their churches in the new "Brain and Soul Boosting for Seniors" (BSBS) programme recently published by Pilgrim's Friend Society. BSBS incorporates cognitive behavioural therapy principles, including guided discovery and the meanings individuals give to events in their lives. A study published by King's College London and the Maudsley NHS Trust showed for the first time that CBT strengthens important connections in the brain and leads to long-term reduction in symptoms and recovery of mental health, and it's long been known that CBT has positive effects in a whole range of applications and that the effects are long-lasting and life-changing.

The BSBS sessions also give spiritual support, and are based on the understanding that God designed human beings to work in relationship with one another, building one another up. Janet ran sessions for nearly three years with different groups of older people. She said, "You could always see individuals' confidence and self-esteem growing, as well as better mental processing. One lady said that for the first time she felt free to talk about things she normally isn't able to." A man who had to be persuaded to join in by his wife, because he said his memory wasn't good enough, changed his mind and found that, because of the way the sessions are structured, he remembered quite a few things, and his self-confidence leapt from zero to ten out of ten.

Group leaders Sally and Jo from Nottingham find that the sense of well-being rises throughout each session. They said, "We have a mixed group including some who are living with dementia. We have created a cosy, comfortable and 'predictable' space in the church where we meet fortnightly on a Friday morning. We have found the predictable and structured nature of the sessions to be very important. It lowers participants' anxiety levels, making them feel safe, and enables them to open up and participate at their own level. The sense of well-being and connection is always greater by the end of a session than at the beginning."

It helps to look for special interests among seniors that can benefit the church as a whole. An 80-year-old who became quite deaf developed a ministry of keeping in touch with missionaries by email, writing a newsletter that the church secretary printed out for distribution to those without computers. Not everyone will come up with ideas at once, but they will over time if they know they will be considered. Many seniors are actively involved in activities organized by the church, for example, lunchtime outreach, or mid-week meetings, or visiting people in the community. In Birmingham, an 82-year-old opens her home to the wives of international visitors for tea and conversation once a week. Another woman in her 80s visits older people in the community who have attended the church's holiday week.

A group of seniors, led by a retired vicar, requested copies of *Worshipping with Dementia* for taking services in housing schemes and care homes. Roger tells of a church known to him that was beginning to decline, so a small group of older members decided to meet to pray specifically that this would reverse and that the congregation would grow. Their families began to comment on their weekly meetings, and one of their daughters came to church to see what it was like. Then another, then another, and in time they brought their friends and some came to know the Lord and, eventually, the congregation was growing and vibrant once again.

Splendour

"Grey hair is a crown of splendour," says Proverbs 16:31 (NIV 2011); "it is found in the way of righteousness." In an earlier book[85] I described meeting a team of mainly older people on a visit to a large church in Bradford, in the north of England. The team, called "Splendour", were committed to reaching out to older people in their community, as well as to caring for the elderly in their own congregation. Their ages ranged from late teens to mid-90s. The oldest member of the team was 95-year-old Gertrude. She had been part of the church from its very early days, and had seen many changes.

Gertrude told me her purpose in life was to encourage communication between the generations, and she said, "I can't do as much as when I was younger, because your body doesn't respond to what you want to do, though God does give me strength to do what I need to do. The church is such a blessing to me and to the young people. I am so happy to see them growing up and to know that when God calls me Home the church is going to be alright. I am so excited about it." Gertrude makes a point of welcoming older people brought in by the minibus from care schemes in the area. Wheelchairs are catered for, and seats are reserved at the front, although people are free to sit where they choose.

They had also inspired the young ones. I heard a group of teenagers practising pieces of music that they would later take into care homes to play to their residents. It was loud, raucous, and full of life. I asked if the residents liked that sort of music. "Well, a lot of them are deaf," replied one of the musicians, "but they like us to go and play." With such an outflow of energy and goodwill, who wouldn't enjoy their company?

Importantly, "Splendour" has the backing of the pastoral team. A few weeks before my visit an 89-year-old man had committed his life to the Lord as the service came to an end. Delighted, the pastor said to the congregation, "It's never too late! The devil thought all these years that he had this one safe in his hands. The devil thinks older people have no interest in the church, and then, at the eleventh hour, the 'Splendour' ministry comes along or some other ministry interested in older people and these people are giving their lives to the Lord. It's just amazing!"

Our seniors are like the disciple in the kingdom of heaven described in Matthew 13:52, "who brings from his storeroom new gems of truth as well as old". Are we creating an atmosphere in which they feel free to share, like the team in Bradford, being supported in being able to serve their purpose?

Older church members can be a bit like the family silver,

which is often kept tucked away in a drawer. But it doesn't have to be like that. Challenging our ageist thinking, encouraging our older saints, involving them, asking for their ideas, reminding them that they have "good works" planned for them by God, and that they are here for a purpose, will make them shine – and we will all benefit.

Psalm 92:12–15 says:

> *But the godly will flourish like palm trees*
> *and grow strong like the cedars of Lebanon.*
> *For they are transplanted to the Lord's own house.*
> *They flourish in the courts of our God.*
> *Even in old age they will still produce fruit;*
> *they will remain vital and green.*
> *They will declare, "The Lord is just!*
> *He is my rock!*
> *There is no evil in Him!"*

We need to up our expectations of old age, both for ourselves and for others, for, as far as God's plan is concerned, *age has everything to do with it.*

Recommended reading

What are older people for? How elders will save the world,
William H. Thomas, 2008, VanderWyk & Burnham,
ISBN 978-1889242200

*Counterclockwise: A Proven Way to Think Yourself Younger
and Healthier*, Ellen Langer, 2010, Hodder Paperbacks,
ISBN 978-0340994764

Making Peace with Your Past, H. Norman Wright, reprinted
2013, Revell, a division of Baker Publishing Group,
ISBN 978-0800752361

Dethroning Mammon: Making Money Serve Grace, Justin
Welby, Archbishop of Canterbury, 2016, Bloomsbury,
ISBN 978-1472929785

Right to Die? Euthanasia, assisted suicide and end-of-life care,
John Wyatt, 2015, IVP, ISBN 978-1783593866

Autobiography of a Yorkshire Christian, Douglas Higgins, 2014,
The Banner of Truth Trust, ISBN 978-1848714885

The Best is Yet To Be, Henry Durbanville, reprinted 1993,
B. McCall Barbour, ISBN 0713200316

CBT for Older People, Ken Laidlaw, 2014, Sage Publications Ltd.,
ISBN 978-1849204606

Notes

1. Arthur Rashap, Jefferson Area Board of Aging.

2. James Hillman, *The Force of Character and the Lasting Life*, New York: Random House, 1999.

3. Douglas Higgins, *Autobiography of a Yorkshire Christian*, Edinburgh: Banner of Truth Trust, 2014.

4. http://www.standard.co.uk/news/woman-105-could-be-oldest-driver-in-britain-6582193.html

5. The *Guardian*, 3 January 2016.

6. Selwyn Hughes, *The Holy Spirit, Our Counsellor*, Farnham: CWR, 2004.

7. Henry Durbanville, *The Best Is Yet To Be*, Edinburgh: B. McCall Barbour, 1950.

8. James Hillman, *The Force of Character and the Lasting Life*, New York: Random House, 1999.

9. William H. Thomas, MD, *What are Older People For? How Elders Will Save the World*, St. Louis, MO: VanderWyk & Burnham, 2007.

10. William H. Thomas, MD, *What are Older People For?*

11. Laura Carstensen, YouTube, https://www.ted.com/talks/laura_carstensen_older_people_are_happier

12. http://www.theatlantic.com/technology/archive/2015/07/supersonic-airplanes-concorde/396698/

13. Robert N. Butler, MD, *The Longevity Revolution: The Benefits and Challenges of Living a Long Life*, New York: PublicAffairs, 2008.

14. Robert N. Butler, MD, *The Longevity Revolution: The Benefits and Challenges of Living a Long Life*.

15. *The Times*, 13 December 2016.

16. http://www.psychologicalscience.org/news/were-only-human/the-new-and-nastier-ageism.html

17. http://www.theinvisiblegorilla.com/gorilla_experiment.html

18. Suzanne O'Sullivan *It's All in Your Head: True Stories of Imaginary Illness*, London: Chatto & Windus, 2016.

19. Barbara Myerhoff, *Number our Days*, New York: Dutton, 1978.

20. Robert N. Butler, MD, *The Longevity Revolution*.

21. http://www.theguardian.com/society/2016/apr/17/britons-at-90-healthier-wiser-indepedent-rich-queen

22. http://www.macmillan.org.uk/Documents/GetInvolved/Campaigns/AgeOldExcuse/AgeOldExcuseReport-MacmillanCancerSupport.pdf

23. http://www.telegraph.co.uk/news/health/12158930/Biggest-annual-rise-in-deaths-for-almost-fifty-years-prompts-warnings-of-crisis-in-elderly-care.html

24. Douglas Higgins, *Autobiography of a Yorkshire Christian*.

25. http://uk.businessinsider.com/bank-of-england-governor-mark-carney-britain-lost-decade-2016-12

26. Neil Howe, "How will Boomers Reshape US Cities?", http://www.governing.com/generations/government-management/gov-how-will-boomers-reshape-cities.html

27. *Telegraph*, 19 July 2016.

28. *Idea* Magazine, September/October 2016.

29. http://www.psychologicalscience.org/news/were-only-human/the-new-and-nastier-ageism.html

30. http://www.telegraph.co.uk/news/health/elder/12037426/Lack-of-respect-for-elderly-may-be-fuelling-Alzheimers-epidemic-warn-scientists.html

31. *The Times* online, 24 May 2009.

32. http://www.usatoday.com/story/travel/flights/2013/04/01/airports-plane-bird-strikes/2043411/

33. http://www.usatoday.com/story/travel/flights/2013/04/01/airports-plane-bird-strikes/2043411/

34. https://www.tripadvisor.co.uk/Attraction_Review-g1475934-d196403-Reviews-Big_Pit_National_Coal_Museum-Blaenavon_Torfaen_South_Wales_Wales.html

35. http://www.wales.nhs.uk/documents/090203historypublichealthen[1].pdf

36. Max Pemberton, *Trust Me, I'm a (Junior) Doctor*, London: Hodder & Stoughton, 2008.

37. http://www.refinery29.uk/2016/04/109663/vogue-uk-harvey

38. The *Daily Telegraph*, 9 November 2016.

39. https://www.theguardian.com/cities/2016/apr/28/teach-young-people-stories-ageing-cities

40. http://www.desiringgod.org/articles/hillary-bernie-donald-and-me

41. Louise Morse, *Dementia: Pathways to Hope*, Oxford: Monarch Books, 2015.

42. *Mature Times*, October 2016.

43. http://www.itv.com/news/calendar/2016-02-24/80-year-old-runner-is-just-5-secs-slower-than-usain-bolt/

44. http://www.mirror.co.uk/news/real-life-stories/silver-sprinter-aged-80-sets-7796131

45. http://www.edinburghnews.scotsman.com/sport/football/hibs/hibs-oldest-fan-sam-martinez-dies-at-age-of-106-1-4211806

46. http://www.dailymail.co.uk/debate/article-3367492/Christians-saved-Nazis-save-greater-evil-Powerful-eloquent-

utterly-gripping-Jewish-peer-96-mission-stop-massacre-innocents.html

47. Ellen Langer, *Counterclockwise: A Proven Way to Think Yourself Younger and Healthier*, London: Hodder & Stoughton, 2010.

48. http://www.child-encyclopedia.com/child-care-early-childhood-education-and-care/according-experts/child-care-and-its-impact-young

49. Jill Bolte Taylor, *My Stroke of Insight*, London: Hodder & Stoughton, 2009.

50. Dr Caroline Leaf, *Who Switched Off My Brain?*, Southlake, TX: Thomas Nelson, 2009.

51. www.nobelprize.org/nobel_prizes/medicine/laureates/2000/kandel-bio.html

52. Tom Kitwood, *Dementia Reconsidered: The Person Comes First)*, Buckingham and Philadelphia: Open University Press, 1997.

53. Ellen Langer, *Counterclockwise*.

54. http://www.dailymail.co.uk/news/article-3182813/Healthy-former-nurse-75-died-Swiss-suicide-clinic-deciding-didn-t-want-risk-burden-family-NHS.html

55. Allan H. Ropper, MD, and Brian D. Burrell, *Reaching Down the Rabbit Hole: A Renowned Neurologist Explains the Mystery and Drama of Brain Disease*, New York: St Martin's Press, 2014.

56. Ellen Langer, *Counterclockwise*.

57. *Mail on Sunday*, Lifestyle, Jn 15, 2017.

58. Atul Gawande, *The Checklist Manifesto: How to Get Things Right*, London: Profile Books, 2011.

59. http://www.theaiatrust.com/whitepapers/ethics/study.php

60. Andrew White, *Faith Under Fire*, Oxford: Monarch Books, 2007.

61. https://www.youtube.com/watch?v=im0F91tUiek

62. James Hillman, *The Force of Character and the Lasting Life*, New York: Random House, 1999.

63. Graham Stokes, *And Still the Music Plays: Stories of People with Dementia*, London: Hawker Publications Ltd, 2010.

64. Lars Tornstam (Social Gerontology Group, Uppsala University, 1973) in William Thomas, *What are Older People For?*, St. Louis, MO: VanderWyk & Burnham, 2007.

65. William Thomas, *What are Older People For?*

66. *The Collected Letters of C. S. Lewis, Volume II: Family Letters 1905–1931*. Copyright © 2004 by C. S. Lewis Pte. Ltd. Used with permission of HarperCollins Publishers.

67. "Trapped in a Bubble", British Red Cross, December 2016, http://www.redcross.org.uk/~/media/BritishRedCross/Documents/What%20we%20do/UK%20services/Co_Op_Trapped_in_a_bubble_report_AW.pdf

68. http://www.dailymail.co.uk/health/article-1298225/Loneliness-killer-Its-bad-health-alcoholism-smoking-eating-say-scientists.html

69. https://www.rush.edu/health-wellness/discover-health/loneliness-and-alzheimers

70. http://www.bible.ca/ef/topical-rehoboam-so-the-king-did-not-listen%20to-the-people.htm

71. http://www.dailymail.co.uk/sciencetech/article-4149092/What-shape-brain-says-you.html

72. http://www.telegraph.co.uk/business/2016/12/05/mark-carney-warns-first-lost-decade-150-years-brands-eurozone/

73. http://www.lifeway.com/Article/pastor-Questioning-heaven – 9 facts about Heaven that will surprise you

74. http://www.spurgeon.org/sermons/2205.php

75. https://www.theguardian.com/society/2015/mar/30/how-why-older-people-valued-knowledge-experience

76. http://www.ageuk.org.uk/latest-news/archive/older-people-contribute-6bn-economy/

77. http://time.com/4327430/baby-boomers-are-isolating-themselves-as-they-age-thats-bad-for-everyone/

78. http://www.cmaj.ca/content/189/3/E101

79. C. S. Lewis, *Mere Christianity*, New York: Macmillan Publishing Co., 1952.

80. Louise Morse, *Dementia: Pathways to Hope*.

81. *Ageing and Society*, 22, pp. 647–663. doi:10.1017/S0144686X02008747.

82. Mark Carney, "The Spectre of Monetarism", speech given at Liverpool John Moores University, 5 December 2016, http://www.bankofengland.co.uk/publications/Documents/speeches/2016/speech946.pdf

83. Justin Welby, *Dethroning Mammon: Making Money Serve Grace*, London: Bloomsbury, 2016.

84. John Telford, *The Life of John Wesley* – Chapter 22, http://wesley.nnu.edu/?id=104

85. Louise Morse, *Could It Be Dementia? Losing Your Mind Doesn't Mean Losing Your Soul*, Oxford: Monarch Books, 2008.